Getting Back to Bethel

A Journey from Religion to Relationship

Dietra Howard-Sherman

Getting Back to Bethel: A Journey from Religion to Relationship
by Dietra Howard-Sherman

Cover design, editing, book layout, and publishing services by KishKnows, Inc., Richton Park, Illinois, 708-252-DOIT
admin@kishknows.com, www.kishknows.com

ISBN 978-1-7329807-0-9
LCCN 2018966289

All rights reserved. No part of this book may be reproduced, distributed, or transmitted in any form or by any means, including photocopying, recording, digital scanning, or other electronic or mechanical methods, without the prior written permission of the publisher, except in the case of brief quotations embodied in critical reviews and certain other noncommercial uses permitted by copyright law. For permission requests, please contact Dietra Howard at dietradhoward@gmail.com.

Some Scripture references may be paraphrased versions or illustrative references of the author. Unless otherwise indicated, all Scripture quotations are taken from the **Holy Bible, New Living Translation (NLT)**, copyright © 1996, 2004, 2015 by Tyndale House Foundation. Used by permission of Tyndale House Publishers, Inc., Carol Stream, Illinois 60188.

All rights reserved.

Scriptures noted as **NKJV** are taken from the **New King James Version**®. Copyright © 1982 by Thomas Nelson. Used by permission. All rights reserved.

Scriptures noted as **ESV** are taken from the **ESV® Bible (The Holy Bible, English Standard Version®)**. ESV® Text Edition: 2016. Copyright © 2001 by Crossway, a publishing ministry

The Talk About "Getting Back to Bethel"...

Prophetess Dietra Howard-Sherman is a woman that God has His hand upon for the salvation of His people in this hour. It's not because she is a member of this ministry; but as I read this book, I felt God speak to me in a such a manner that it set my spirit on a quest to experience Him in a new and greater way. The contents of this book are without question "God-inspired" and it is well-suited for all of the household of faith. This book tugs at the "reins of my heart" and encourages me to know God in a greater way. I often wondered why I wasn't satisfied with the status quo or religion. My heart is on fire to experience God at Bethel, for no other place can compare.

This book is a "game-changer" as we look around us, because we know that the contents are true and accurate. There is a hunger and thirst for more than what we are accustomed to, and it is written for all who are serious, and tired of dry, routine, non-Holy Spirit-driven services. I plead with you to just open and read, and allow the Spirit of God to take you on the journey of a lifetime…a journey that you've prayed, fasted and waited for.

Some books, by design, are written to encourage, instruct, and teach success, but I genuinely believe that *this* book will revolutionize your life. I would challenge anyone who has ever experienced delays, setbacks, and failures to try "living in Bethel." One can hardly live where God lives—the Holy of Holies, beyond the veil—and not have their life be greatly impacted.

As a pastor, I've been stirred to prayer, telling God, *"I see what You've been telling me all along. I know why my soul wasn't satisfied, but longed for greater. 'IT'S BETHEL.'"*

~Elder Lowell T. James, Pastor
Anderson Memorial COGIC
High Springs, FL

I found this book to be a very soul-shaking encounter. As you travel with Jacob on his journey, you can feel the uneasiness in his soul. You *become* Jacob. This book encouraged me to take a long, hard, honest look at how we really see our relationship with God. Why do we do what we do? Is the God that we know the God of the Bible...or is He a god that we have "conjured up" through vain philosophies, traditions, and rituals? This book made me realize just how deeply rooted my religious ideologies were. I felt uncomfortable, offended, and challenged, and I was forced to look at how I felt as I carried out religious practices garbed in what appeared to be a righteous relationship.

The process of the making of Jacob into Israel will encourage you to align yourself with the God of the Bible and not the one you made up from pieces of unbiblical information passed down unwittingly from others, or from the information that you have selfishly interpreted on your own. This book comes out of the gate asking the question *"Why?"*

While watching a documentary about the Kennedys one night, I paid close attention to an interview that Roger Mudd did with the Democratic nominee, then-Senator Ted Kennedy, in 1979. Senator Kennedy was a shoe-in for the Democratic nomination; and according to many, would be the next President of the United States. During the interview, Mudd asked a very simple, pointed, and penetrating question that demanded nothing but honesty: *"Why do you want to be President?"*

Senator Kennedy seemed stunned. It was as if he had never really considered the question of *why* he was running for the highest office in the United States of America. Was it because of his brothers, former President John F. Kennedy and former Presidential candidate Robert F. Kennedy? Was he just doing what was expected, or did he have a more personal reason? Was he just trying to carry on a tradition? Senator Kennedy fumbled at that question in front of the whole world—and eventually ended up withdrawing from the race.

Getting Back to Bethel is like interviewing with Roger Mudd. *"Why do you do what you do?"* It will make you uncomfortable and challenge the very core of who God is to you, and what it means to be His child. It will show you the way *back to Bethel*.

> *~ First Lady Brenda James*
> *Anderson Memorial COGIC*
> *High Springs, FL*

of Good News Publishers. The ESV® text has been reproduced in cooperation with and by permission of Good News Publishers. Unauthorized reproduction of this publication is prohibited. All rights reserved.

Copyright © 2018 by Dietra Howard-Sherman

Printed in the United States of America

From the Author...

Getting "Back to Bethel," the place where we first encounter Abba, our Father, is a simple declaration to make—but a difficult journey to complete when we are entangled with the spirit of religion. Once we make the decision to fulfill our God-given destiny and get back to Bethel, the enemy knows that he does not have the power to stop us, so he attempts to hold us in spiritual locations such as Haran, Gilead, Manheim, Peniel, Succoth, and Shechem. These delays are designed to keep us from reaching Bethel and dwelling in the presence of God.

Jacob endured a lot on his journey of getting back to Bethel, but he also learned a lot. The journey that we take to get to Bethel is a part of our testimony to let others know that it is possible to live a life where we are constantly dwelling in the presence of Abba, our Father, and operating in our day-to-day tasks. I am forever grateful for the ministry of Prophetess Sophia Ruffin and Prophetess Devon Mays because they walked through their journey and are now dwelling in Bethel. They have encouraged not only me but others in my church to get "back to Bethel." It is my prayer that this book will encourage you to complete your journey and get to Bethel...and when you get there, don't forget to go back and share your testimony so that you may also encourage someone else to complete their journey. Remember... the enemy is defeated by the blood of the Lamb and the word of our testimonies!

Table of Contents

Dedication xv
A Special Thank-You xvii
Prologue 1
Introduction 3

Chapter 1:
Haran: The "Dry Places" 15

Chapter 2:
Gilead: Deliverance from the "Rocky Places" 23

Chapter 3:
Mahanaim:
Deliverance from Double-Minded Thinking 35

Chapter 4:
Peniel: The Struggle Within 43

Chapter 5:
Succoth: Under the Shelter of His Wings 57

Chapter 6:
Shechem: Journey Out of the Comfortable Places ... 65

Chapter 7:
Bethel: Returning to Our God 73

Conclusion 81

About the Author 83

Contact the Author 85

"Jacob set up a stone pillar to mark the place where God had spoken to him. Then he poured wine over it as an offering to God and anointed the pillar with olive oil. And Jacob named the place Bethel (which means "house of God"), because God had spoken to him there."
Genesis 35:14-15 (NLT)

Dedication

I lovingly dedicate this book in memory of my father, Deacon Calvin Howard, who taught me through his actions the importance of starting your day off with a prayer; and in memory of my mother, Virginia Howard, who taught me that the answer to every problem that I would ever face is found in the Word of God.

To my spiritual parents, Superintendent Elder Lowell T. James and District Missionary Brenda James, I would like to thank you for teaching me through your actions how to become a living epistle of Christ. I am forever grateful that Abba entrusted my spiritual destiny to be birthed through the ministry of Anderson Memorial COGIC, High Springs, FL.

A Special Thank-You

To my husband, Greg. Thank you for loving me, sitting up with me into the wee hours of the morning while I wrote, making sure that my coffee supply never ran out, and praying for me. I love you!

To my children: Brannon, Deonte, Dayonna, Michael, Caitlyn, and Joviel. Thank you for your words of encouragement and prayers.

To my first grandchild, Carter Lee. God blessed me with you at a time when I was about to give up. XOXOXO

To my personal intercessors: my sisters Labrisha, Belita, and Joyce. Thank you for your words of encouragement, and for interceding and petitioning heaven on my behalf.

To my family and friends that I did not mention by name… Thank you.

Abba, Father, I release a prayer for the one who is holding this book in their hands. Father, I am glad that when I pray, You hear me. I pray that every form of religion and tradition, and every preconceived notion that they carry in their heart, mind, and spirit that is an incorrect representation of who You are and what You want to perform in their lives be removed by the time they complete this book. Abba, Father, I pray that those incorrect ideologies be replaced with true knowledge and understanding of the power of who You are, and that they will be able to operate in the pure power and authority that You have given them as a believer to wreak havoc on our adversary, the devil, and bring the manifestation of the Kingdom to their homes, families, churches, cities, and regions, and in every aspect of their lives. Abba, Father, I ask these things in Jesus' name. Amen.

Prologue

When reading about Jacob in the Book of Genesis, one often mistakenly assumes that Jacob's journey to Bethel started in **Genesis 28,** when he received orders from his father to go to Pandin Aram and obtain a wife from among his mother's people. In actuality, Jacob's journey began in his mother's womb. Just as it is with you and I, the plans for Jacob's life were ordained by God before he was even birthed into this world.

While in the womb, Jacob and his brother, Esau, struggled with each other so much that it caused their mother, Rebekah, to ask God what was taking place inside of her. God then revealed the plan for Jacob's life to his mother; plans for Jacob to be the stronger twin, and to rule over his brother **(Genesis 25:22-23)**. Even in the womb, Jacob knew that there was a place that God had called him to, and that it was worth fighting for. After the birth of Jacob and his brother, Rebekah took it upon herself to "help" Jacob fulfill the destiny to which God had called him, but because of her limited knowledge of who God was, she only made Jacob's journey to his destiny longer and harder than what God had intended it to be.

> *How often do we, like Rebekah, try to "help God out" and only end up complicating the process?*

This is exactly what is happening in churches that are stuck in tradition. Because they do not fully understand who God is, they limit Him to movement through traditional and religious actions, instead of being led by God Himself through the power of the Holy Spirit, whose indwelling in us leads us into a personal relationship with Abba. We need a relationship that is built on Godly encounters, not religious activities or traditions. The purpose of this book is to remind us that before we were formed in our mother's womb, God set us apart and called us to fulfill the destiny that He has ordained for us *(Jeremiah 1:5)*...and with this calling comes opposition from the enemy.

The "Spirit of Religion"

We must understand that it is the enemy's job to keep us from reaching our God-ordained destiny, and that one of the most effective ways that he has of doing this is through the "spirit of religion." The way that this spirit operates is by allowing us to *think* we are in relationship with God when we are really *far away* from Him. It is through the spirit of religion and condemnation that the enemy keeps us from the freedom of a personal relationship with Abba, our Father.

There is a place where God dwells, and He wants us to dwell there with Him. God has released great revelation through Jacob's journey on how we can be set free from the bondage of religion and get to the place where He dwells...so let's *Get Back to Bethel*!

Introduction

As the "church," we have become one of the world's largest participants in ritualistic behaviors, meaning that we attend church without the expectation of God's glory to be manifested. We "know" exactly how many songs the choir is going to sing; how long praise and worship "should" last, and when the announcements are going to be made. We treat church like the social event of the week, instead of it being a gathering place where the Glory of God can be manifested, and the people of God can gather together to be encouraged, strengthened, and empowered to succeed. It is not God's desire for us to go to church every Sunday and become so focused on the order of service that we do not allow Him to move as He desires. God wants to be in a *real, authentic* relationship with us. He wants to engage in the same kind of intimate interactions that we share with those closest to us.

Even though I "knew" this in my head, my heart and actions were not reflective of this mindset. I have never thought of myself as being "religious." In fact, I was one of those people who constantly voiced my objections to religious practices and denominational traditions. But then God and I embarked on a journey, and I discovered that the spirit of religion had a tight grip on me…and it was one that the enemy was not willing to let go of easily.

Going Through the Motions

The "spirit of religion" would have us believing that we are defeating the kingdom of darkness by attending church—but Satan is not intimidated just because we attend church services, programs, and every conference that we can. But what intimidates him is Believers having a *true, intimate relationship* that reveals God to us as Abba, our Father. The term *journey* means *"the act of traveling from one location to another."* God took me from a place where the spirit of religion held me captive, to the place where He dwells.

The journey to escape from the spirit of religion is not as easy as changing churches. It's not our *physical* location, but rather the location of our *hearts* that is important. There is no way that we can move from religion to relationship without our hearts being totally committed to Abba, our Father. It's important to understand that the only way we can escape the grip of religion is to have our hearts turned toward God, so that our participation in these same practices becomes a "God encounter" instead of a "religious and ritualistic" service.

The danger of being in the grip of religion is that it can have a hold on us before we know what has happened. Our adversary is very strategic in launching this attack. Many of us become so ritualistic in our time and behaviors with Abba, our Father, and honestly feel as if we are "honoring" God because we are "going through the motions" of worship, prayer, and praise. What we fail to realize is that even though our *bodies* are present, our *hearts* are elsewhere.

The Heart of the Matter

In **1 Samuel 16:7**, God tells Samuel that **"Man looks at the outer appearance, but God looks at the heart,"** and this is the guideline that determines whether or not our actions of prayer and worship are genuine or merely ritualistic, (which means they hold no heart value) making them worthless to God.

Introduction

The grip of religion is most prevalent in those of us who have been raised in the "church" and have become accustomed to the culture of the church, through our denominational (or non-denominational) associations, our families, and those in our communities.

When we are in the grip of religion, we genuinely believe that we have fellowship with God—but in reality, what we have is a fraudulent relationship that is built on a sandy foundation. This is truly a dangerous place to dwell, because while we are in this place, it is impossible to experience a pure relationship with Abba…one that is built on a solid foundation that releases a worship of spirit and truth.

The Birthright

> **Birthright:** *The special rights and privileges of honor that were given to the first-born male in a Jewish family. These rights and privileges included receiving a double portion of the father's inheritance and giving the oldest son judicial authority over family matters.*

Jacob's journey is an interesting one. From the beginning, we are able to see that the spirit of religion is working behind the scenes in his life.

According to Jewish tradition, the birthright belonged to the oldest son. Esau was the oldest son, which placed him in the honored position of being the recipient of the family's birthright. I believe that while Jacob and Esau were in their mother's womb, Esau was already in position to be born first; but because of God's calling on his life, Jacob was fighting for position and attempting to become, in effect, the firstborn son. It would have seemed that once Jacob received his brother's birthright that he was walking in his God-ordained calling, but because God is Spirit, He institutes and dictates from the spiritual realm, then manifests His plans in the natural.

I Corinthians 2:14 tells us that the natural man does not receive the things from God's Spirit, because it is "foolish" to him. Therefore, one of the key strategies of the spirit of religion is to try and get the believer to see and operate through the "natural" or "fleshly" mindset. In doing this, the believer is now limited in what they can comprehend instead of being led by the Holy Spirit. But God never deals with us according to the "natural" or "fleshly" means. God deals with our spirit. Jacob receiving Esau's birthright was not the spiritual plan of God; but instead, it was a (poor) substitute for what God had really ordained for Jacob, which was the manifestation of his spiritual birthright rather than his natural one.

"Helping God Out"

With the "help" of his mother, and through his own actions, Jacob not only ends up with his brother's birthright, but he also tricks his father into bestowing upon him the blessing that Isaac wanted to give to Esau. It is because of these experiences that Jacob finds himself on a journey to Haran, his mother's homeland. While traveling to his destination, Jacob encounters God, and he calls the place *"Bethel," "The place where God dwells."*

At sundown, he arrived at a good place to set up camp and stopped there for the night. Jacob found a stone to rest his head against and lay down to sleep. As he slept, he dreamed of a stairway that reached from the earth up to heaven. And he saw the angels of God going up and down the stairway. At the top of the stairway stood the LORD, and he said, 'I am the LORD, the God of your grandfather, Abraham and the God of your father, Isaac. The ground you are laying on belongs to you. I am giving it to you and your descendants. Your descendants will be as numerous as the dust of the earth! They will spread out in all directions-to the west and the east, to the north and the south. And all the families of the earth will be blessed through you and your descendants. What's more, I am with you and I will protect you wherever you go. One day, I will bring you back to this land. I will not leave you until I have finished giving you everything I promised you.' Then Jacob awoke from his sleep and said, 'Surely the LORD is in this place, and I wasn't even aware of it.' But he was also afraid and said 'What an awesome place this is! It is none other than the house of God, the very gateway to heaven!' The next morning Jacob got up very early. He took the stone he had rested his head against, and he set it upright as a memorial pillar then he poured olive oil over it. He named that place Bethel which means 'House of God'... Genesis 28:11-19 (NLT)

It is important to understand that while in the womb, Jacob didn't have the interference of family and culture to hinder that which God had placed inside of him. The only directive that he had at that time came directly from God, and Jacob fought to gain his God-ordained position as ruler over his brother. It is not until God reveals His intentions for Jacob to Rebekah that we see cultural and family influences attempt to hinder Jacob's God-given destiny.

Because Rebekah trusted in other gods, she didn't have a real understanding of the true living God—the God of her husband. She didn't understand that when God speaks, it is not just limited to the natural realm, but that it is the authority in the spiritual realm as well. Since she did not understand this, Rebekah thought that by "helping" Jacob receive Esau's birthright and blessings, the plan of God would be fulfilled. She took it upon herself to "help God out."

The "Natural" Mindset

This is what we see happening in the churches today, where the spirit of religion is holding God's people captive to a natural mindset. In doing this, the spirit keeps the believers limited to what they see in the natural, which in turn means they are engaging in a shallow relationship with Abba, our Father. When we limit the depths of our relationship with Abba to "the shallows," we cannot operate in our mandated authority, nor can the greater works that Jesus spoke of in *John 14* be manifest. The only way to be released from a natural mindset is to dwell in Bethel, the place where God lives. Dwelling in Bethel produces a spiritual mindset which produces an atmosphere for our God given authority to rule.

On his journey to and from Haran, Jacob passes through some very significant places. We will be focusing on Gilead, Mahanaim, Peniel, Succoth, and Shechem. God has revealed to me the relationship between Jacob's physical journey (getting back to Bethel) and our spiritual journey. He showed me how many believers were on their way to dwelling with Him in Bethel but have become "spiritually stuck" in places such as Haran, Mahanaim, and Succoth…places that God has not ordained for us. The most disheartening thing is that *we don't even realize* that we are dwelling in strange lands.

One of the reasons that we don't realize it is because these are places where God will often visit us, and where we may have genuine encounters with Him. These encounters usually occur when we are thirsty, and have a deep, spiritual need for God to move on our behalf. Because He is a just and loving God, He will meet us where we are. He allows us to experience His presence, but *He will not dwell there, nor does He desire for us to remain in these places.*

A "Hostage" Situation

We must realize that these are temporary locations, and the only place that He will dwell with us is in Bethel. Because of the influence of the church culture, we often make the tragic mistake of trying to hold Abba, our Father, "hostage" in these temporary locations.

We hold Him hostage by trying to get Him to show up and respond the same way in every circumstance of our lives. For instance, if we experienced His presence like never before while we were crying out on our knees in the middle of a worship service, then we can make the mistake of expecting God to show up this way all the time. Worship that was once sincere and heartfelt has now become ritualistic, which in turn leaves us feeling disappointed and void because God doesn't reveal Himself like He did the first time.

I know you may be thinking, "That's ludicrous," but think about the last time you experienced God's presence and were moved to true worship. How many times have you tried to recapture that moment by doing the exact same thing you were doing at the time God revealed Himself?

Holy *Appearance*...Shallow *Experience*

Attending church services today has become, for many, one of the most "ritualistic" things that we do. Services are "program-oriented," and God *never intended* for us to get "caught up" like that. We as a culture put more emphasis on practicing such things so that we may appear to be holy, and in doing so, we often get caught up in the behavior of what we are *doing* instead of remembering why (and who) we are *worshiping*. When we engage in such behaviors, we are engaging in a shallow experience with Abba the Father...an experience which keeps the power of God from producing greater works in our lives.

Getting Back to Bethel

I had no idea that I was stuck in these temporary spiritual locations. These were places where God had not ordained for me to remain and places where God Himself did not dwell. Because I felt His presence with me, and He visited me often in those places, I assumed that those were the places where He was and where He wanted me to be.

It wasn't until I encountered the ministry of Prophetess Sophia Ruffin that I realized that I was stuck, and that I was nowhere near entering Bethel—let alone dwelling there. It was through watching her ministry and the teaching and lifestyle of my spiritual parents, Superintendent Lowell T. James and District Missionary Brenda James, that I was able to experience the presence of God, the power and authority of God that I had heard the older saints in the church testify about, and the God of the Bible that I had read about. I now understood that the only way to experience God's power, presence, and authority in my life on that level was to live in the place where God dwells.

My experience with the power and authority in which Prophetess Ruffin operated resembled nothing that I had ever seen in a ministry during my walk with God; in fact, her ministry was the total opposite of the "boxed religion" in which I held God's power and authority. It was through watching her on Periscope that I realized that fellowship with God could consist of truth, freedom, and boldness to be who God was calling me to be and still be authentic and Holy. It was through following her ministry that my spiritual eyes were opened, and I realized that I was "spiritually stuck" in religious, traditional behaviors. Although these behaviors allowed God to *visit* me, they did not allow God and I to *dwell together*, which is the only way that we can effectively operate in the power and authority that God has given us as believers.

Introduction

If you are not experiencing the "greater works" that Jesus spoke of in *John 14*, then God has led you to this book as a means to get you to the place that He ordained for you before you were formed in your mother's womb. As you read the pages, allow the power of the Holy Spirit to speak to you, and to reveal to you where you are on your journey to Bethel.

Listen For His Voice

You may discover that you are dwelling in several of the locations mentioned in this book, or you may be stuck in one location. Whatever the case may be, allow God to speak to you and to purge you of the preconceived notions that people and your surroundings have dictated to you about who Abba the Father is, and who He has called you to be. I pray that God will move you from your temporary dwelling place to your God-ordained position…Bethel *"The place where God dwells."* Come journey with me as we expose the enemy for who he is and get you to the place where God has ordained for you to dwell.

As men and women of God, we believe by faith that this world is not our final home and that one day, when we transition from earthly labor to our heavenly reward, we will live forever in the presence of God. Although this belief is correct, what many of us fail to realize is that Abba, our Father, has made provision for us to dwell with Him in this earthly world.

The Hebrew meaning for Bethel is *"House of God, the place where God dwells, the Holy of Holies."* There was a time when access to the presence of God was reserved for only certain individuals…most notably Moses, Abraham, Isaiah, Jeremiah, and the priestly line of Aaron…but through the death and resurrection of Jesus Christ, that access was made available to everyone who believes in the work of the cross.

He is the Mercy Seat of Sacrifice

*"And Jesus cried out again with a loud voice
and yielded up His spirit.
Then behold, the veil of the temple
was torn in two from top to bottom..."
Matthew 27:50-51 (NKJV)*

When Jesus died on the cross, He became the mercy seat of sacrifice, and it was no longer necessary for the high priest to make the yearly sacrifice of atonement on behalf of the people. Access to the Holy of Holies was now available for all who believe in the life, death, and resurrection of Jesus Christ, our Savior.

"And so, dear brothers and sisters, we can boldly enter Heaven's Most Holy Place because of the blood of Jesus. By his death, Jesus opened a new and life-giving way through the curtain into the Most Holy Place and since we have a great High Priest who rules over God's house, let us go right into the presence of God with sincere hearts fully trusting him. For our guilty consciences have been sprinkled with Christ's blood to make us clean, and our bodies have been washed with pure water." Hebrews 10:19-22 (NLT)

It is through the blood of Jesus Christ that we have gained access to the presence of Abba, our Father, and that access is not limited to "chance encounters," or reserved for when we transition to our Heavenly home. We are able to be in the presence of God...to live where He lives in Bethel. Now that we know that we have been granted the privilege of residing in Bethel while living in our earthly bodies, let's begin our journey and *Get Back to Bethel.*

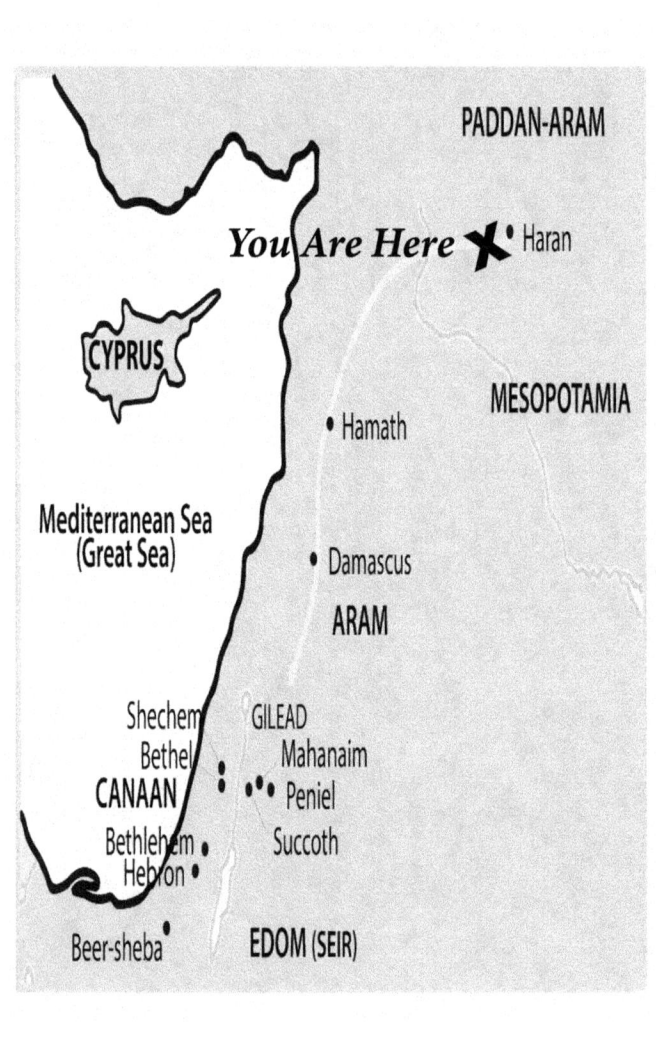

Chapter 1

Haran:
The "Dry Places"

When we make the decision to accept Christ as our Lord and Savior, we embark on a journey of getting to know Him… and getting to know ourselves. For those of us raised in the church, we may not have been given the choice to attend church—it was a given that we would be there. For those of us who didn't "join" a church but were instead "born into one," we often find ourselves struggling with our birthright…the right to be *nothing more* and *nothing less* than who God has designed us to be.

> *"'For I know the plans I have for you,' says the Lord. 'They are plans for good and not for disaster, to give you a future and a hope.'"*
> *Jeremiah 29:11 (NLT)*

God has the plan and blueprint for our lives, but when we are born into the church, that plan and blueprint can easily become altered by those with even the best of intentions for us. This happens when more emphasis is put on religion and tradition than on our personal relationship with Abba, our Father. It leaves us in a parched and dry place in our relationship with Him, and thus we find ourselves dwelling in Haran.

The Danger of Spiritual Dehydration

Haran means *"parched,"* which is defined as *"dehydrated; extremely, excessively, or completely dry."* To find ourselves in

Haran means that we are spiritually dry and dehydrated. In the natural world, dehydration is very dangerous and can lead to death. The same holds true spiritually—when we are spiritually dehydrated, we are in danger of spiritual death. If you find yourself stuck and not able to flourish in the things of God, you very well may be "stuck" in the dry, parched land of Haran. The only way to escape Haran is to allow for the living waters of God to overflow into every area of your life.

When it was agreed upon that Jacob should leave his family, he found himself in the land of Haran. His very first experience in this land was witnessing the watering of the flocks.

"So Jacob went on his journey and came to the land of the people of the East. And he looked and saw a well in the field; and behold, there were three flocks of sheep lying by it; for out of that well they watered the flocks. A large stone was on the well's mouth. Now all the flocks would be gathered there; and they would roll the stone from the well's mouth, water the sheep, and put the stone back in its place on the well's mouth."
Genesis 29:1-3 (NKJV)

Open Field-Closed Well

Jacob came upon this well in an open field, much like when we first come to Christ. We are so excited and open to the possibility that God wants to be in relationship with us. In spite of everything that we have experienced—the good, the bad, and the ugly— God still wants an intimate relationship we us, but then we are quickly introduced to the spirit of religion, through the operation of others who have been "in the church" longer then we have.

This spirit will often reveal itself by attacking the way we pray or dress, or even the way we choose to praise and worship God. The spirit of religion will quickly remind us that the only time we can drink from the well is during the watering of the flock, which in many instances is listed somewhere in the order of service, or is evident in the way "things are done" at church.

The spirit of religion controls the stone. When we first come to Christ, we are thirsty. We desire to drink from the well of Abba's presence all the time—not just when the stone is rolled away. But because the goal of the spirit of religion is to keep us from experiencing the manifestation of God's glory, it will remove the stone, let us take small sips and then just before the glory of God is released in the atmosphere, this spirit quickly rolls the stone back in place to hinder the presence of God from flowing freely. It quickly informs us that it is not "acceptable" to just drink from the fountain of life whenever we want to.

Haran is parched: a dry and thirsty place. This is exactly what religion does to us. It will treat the men and women of God exactly like the sheep were treated in this passage. Think about it this way: Just as the sheep were led to the well, those of us who were "born into the church" have been led to the well of Abba's presence by others, such as parents, grandparents, or others who told us *what* well to go to, *when* to go to it, and *how* we should present ourselves when we go.

The sheep waited for the stone to be rolled back, then they were watered, and the stone was replaced. In many church services, it is dictated to us when we can drink from the presence of Abba, and once the allotted time to drink or be watered has passed, the stone is put back over the well and we are led away. Spiritually, we are taught how to remove and replace a stone over our hearts that hinders us from freely engaging in true worship.

From Religion to Relationship

If we don't take the time to develop a relationship with God that is built on the foundation of spirit and truth, we will find our spiritual life parched, thirsting for more. The journey from *religion* to *relationship* begins in Haran. When we are thirsty, we have two choices. If we sit and do nothing, we will eventually die from dehydration. We have the power, however, to "get up and move," and find something to quench our thirst. The same holds true spiritually. The spirit of religion hopes that we will sit and do nothing, so that we eventually succumb to spiritual dehydration. But the reason you have this book in your hands is because Abba Father is calling you to *move*! His words to you are, *"Why sit ye here and die?"*

Our thirst has caused us to set out on a journey, and Abba Father will be faithful to bring us to a place that is flowing with living water. He is calling us to reside in Bethel…the place where He dwells. He will meet us at the well…all we have to do is show up, and He will meet us there, just as He met the Samaritan woman.

"A woman of Samaria came to draw water. Jesus said to her, 'Give me a drink.' For His disciples had gone away into the city to buy food. Then the woman of Samaria said to Him, 'How is it that you being a Jew, ask a drink from me, a Samaritan woman?' For Jews have no dealings with Samaritans.' Jesus answered and said to her, 'If you knew the gift of God, and who it is who says to you, 'Give me a drink,' you would have asked Him and He would have given you living water.' The woman said to Him, 'Sir. You have nothing to draw with and the well is deep. Where then do you get that living water? Are you greater than our father Jacob, who gave us the well, and drank from it himself, as well as his sons and his livestock?' Jesus answered and said to her, 'Whoever drinks of this water will thirst again, but whoever drinks of the water that I shall give him will never

thirst. But the water that I shall give him will become in him a fountain of water springing up into everlasting life.' The woman said to Him, 'Sir, give me this water, that I may not thirst, nor come here to draw.'"
John 4:7-15 (NKJV)

If we are to ever leave the parched place of Haran, we must first be willing to cross over barriers that have been put in place through man-made traditions. Jesus did not let the fact that the woman was a Samaritan stop Him from interacting with her, and just as Jesus was willing to move past the cultural barrier between Jews and Samaritans, we have to be willing to move beyond the barriers of non-biblical traditions, such as women having to wear white on the First Sunday, or not being allowed to wear pants, or being forbidden to preach from the pulpit.

> *Please hear my heart—the problem is not with the traditions...***the problem is when we condemn ourselves to hell for not participating in them!**

Trying to follow man-made protocols will *always* leave us thirsting for the living water. We were created to be in relationship with *God*, not *religion*. Because it is not Abba's desire for us to dwell in Haran, He will intervene, either by way of a divine encounter directly with Him, or through someone who is in intimate relationship with Him. During this intervention, we need to respond like the Samaritan woman did, and ask Jesus to give us the living water!

If we are going to ever leave the parched lands of Haran, it starts with the living water...*which is the Holy Spirit*. To drink the "living water" that Jesus was referring to is to be led by the Holy Spirit. It is through the *power of the Holy Spirit* that we are transformed from religion to relationship.

Time for Reflection...

-Rebekah wanted to make sure that Jacob received his due, and so she tried to "help God out," and ended up creating a pretty big problem. Can you think of a time where you weren't sure that God could "handle it," and so you decided (or someone decided for you) to "help Him out?" What happened? Did things work out as you hoped?

-Are there traditions or practices that you have grown up with in the church that may have hindered your walk with the Lord? What were they? Have you found a way to move past them, or do you still feel like they are a stumbling block in your walk of faith?

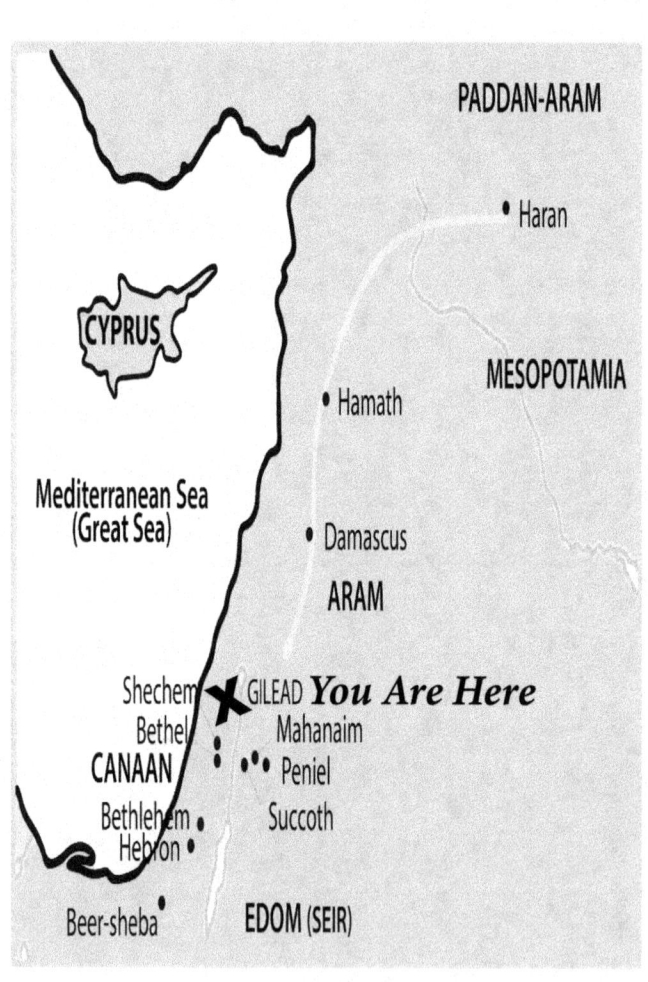

Chapter 2

Gilead: Deliverance from the Rocky Places

Gilead was located between the Jordan and Bashan Rivers, and was known for its rugged terrain. The Biblical meaning of *Gilead* is *"hill of testimony"* or *"mound of testimony."* It is very important to note that the place where God chose for Jacob to finally stand up to Laban was known for its physical characteristics. It was an extremely hilly, rocky, rough territory. When God is calling us to journey from the spirit of religion to relationship, we must understand that *the most rugged place we are going to have to face is the bondage of non-biblical traditions or religious practices that satisfy our flesh.*

While we are on this journey, it is extremely important that we realize that there is a difference between *religion* and the *spirit of religion*. Religion is usually associated with our beliefs and religious behaviors that join us to a group of people who share the same beliefs and behaviors. The *spirit of religion* is present when our pure biblical religion becomes tainted by ungodly motives and influences and/or attempts to replace the work of the Holy Spirit.

The Bondage of Tradition

"Don't let anyone capture you with empty philosophies and high-sounding nonsense that come from human thinking and from the spiritual powers of this world, rather than from Christ."
Colossians 2:8 (NLT)

Getting Back to Bethel

This Scripture is warning us against operating in the spirit of religion. It tells us not to fall captive to the philosophy and traditions of men when they do not align with the Word of God. To become captive means *"to become enslaved or dominated by the captor."* This is exactly what happened to Jacob—he fell victim to the trickery of his uncle. Laban is a perfect example of how the spirit of religion uses trickery and deceit to hold the believer captive. According to **Genesis 31:38**, Jacob remained in bondage to the deceitful lies and tricks of his father-in-law, Laban, for *twenty years*. Laban was able to hold Jacob captive for so long because of traditional practices.

Because Laban did not serve the living true God, his practices and traditions were inspired by ungodly influences. But remember—God had ordained Jacob's destiny from the womb. He never stopped operating on Jacob's behalf, and He continued to orchestrate circumstances that would open Jacob's spiritual eyes and ears so that he could hear the call to go back to Bethel. **Genesis 31:13** tells us that Jacob saw an angel in a dream and heard the call that beckoned him to return to the land of his birth. It is my belief that the phrase "land of his birth" is referring not only to a *physical* location but to a *spiritual* one as well. Abba Father was calling Jacob to the place where his destiny was birthed…which was in His presence. Throughout Scripture, we are reminded that before we are ever formed, God knows us. Indeed, **Jeremiah 1:5** tells us that *before we were even formed in our mother's womb,* Abba, our Father, sanctified us and set us apart for a purpose. Jeremiah also reminds us that **"He knows the plans he has for us, plans for us to prosper and to bring us to an expected end."**

> *Our obedience to our destiny does not require the permission of anyone other than ourselves.*

"Jacob stole away, unknown to Laban the Syrian, in that he did not tell him that he intended to flee. So, he fled with all that he had. He arose and crossed the river and headed toward the mountains of Gilead."
Genesis 31: 20-21 (NKJV)

Crossing the Mountain

Jacob did not tell Laban he was leaving; and when Laban learned of Jacob's departure, he pursued him and caught up with him in Gilead. This is symbolic of what happens to us when we are on the journey from the spirit of religion to relationship. When we make up our mind to have a real relationship with Abba, our Father, we will encounter some mountainous terrains that must be conquered before we can cross over to Bethel, the place where God dwells. When looking at Jacob and Laban's relationship, we see that Laban took advantage of Jacob and the favor that was on his life. He used Jacob so that his household and terrain could prosper. We know this to be true because in **Genesis 30:29-30**, Jacob tells Laban that the only reason his wealth has increased greatly is because the Lord has blessed him through Jacob's hand.

When we are dwelling in a spiritual Gilead, we allow the blessings and favor that are attached to our lives to become used for the selfish intentions of others, instead of letting them glorify Abba, our Father.

Laban was successful at taking advantage of the favor on Jacob's life because he appealed to Jacob's flesh. The same is true when we become entangled with the spirit of religion instead of seeking a relationship with Abba the Father. When we are operating under the influence of the spirit of religion, we will prostitute our gifts and allow others to do the same just so we can satisfy our fleshly desires (or someone else's). When we start to appease our flesh, it weakens and taints our testimony to the holiness and truth of Abba, our Father.

> *"And many will follow their sensuality, and because of them the way of truth will be blasphemed." 2 Peter 2:2 (ESV)*

A crucial mistake that we often make when dwelling in Gilead is that we equate *God's approval* with *fleshly gratification.*

> *Just because our flesh is satisfied **does not mean that God is satisfied with us.***

I have experienced this all too often in the culture of the church. Think about this. If we attend a church service and everyone is dancing and shouting, then we equate that with God's approval and experiencing a "good" church service. *However...*when the church service does not cause people to dance and shout, or move us emotionally, we often feel as though the presence of God was "not there," because the people were not moved into an outward expression of worship. *It is extremely important that we understand that on this journey, we must learn not to associate either God's presence or the absence thereof with an outward display of actions, especially when we are conquering the land of Gilead.*

A Matter of the Heart

Let us remember what God told Samuel when he was to anoint a new king from among Jesse's sons: **"People judge by outward appearances, but the Lord looks at the heart."** We must know that Abba's presence is not predicated on whether we *feel* His presence or not...it's a matter of our *hearts*. We know that He is always with us and He promises through His Word that He will never leave us nor forsake us. We see this to be true in Jacob's life because even though Jacob was not dwelling where God was, God's hand of favor was still upon him, which was evident by the way his Uncle Laban, prospered materialistically by the work of Jacob's hands.

The enemy knows that when we have received the gift of salvation through the works of Christ on the cross, there is nothing he can do to stop it; so, his next step is to hinder us from fulfilling our God-ordained destinies, through hindrances and destruction caused by the spirit of religion. Just as Laban used deceit and trickery to keep Jacob in bondage and use him for his own personal gain, the enemy also desires to keep as many Christians as possible in bondage to the spirit of religion.

As I mentioned earlier, I was born and raised in the church, so I have witnessed the spirit of religion active in the lives of many believers, as well as in my own life. The danger is that what a lot of us consider a personal relationship with Abba is mixed with philosophies, traditions, beliefs, and mindsets that are inspired by others who are seeking to glorify themselves and not Abba, our Father. *Matthew 5:16* tells us to *"... let your good deeds shine out for all to see, so that everyone will praise your heavenly Father."* (NLT) We are called to shine for God and not ourselves!

The key to leaving Gilead is the ability to hear the voice of God and to break free from the spirit of religion by leaving behind every non-biblical teaching and practice that we have ever participated in, walking into the freedom of a loving relationship with Abba the Father, and standing on His promises to us for our God-given destiny. This sounds a lot easier than it actually is!

The Price We Pay to Leave

When Jacob packed up everything he had and left behind a life that he had become accustomed to, his uncle was furious and pursued him. The same will hold true for you and I when we make the decision to leave behind non-biblical traditions, teachings and relationships. It is going to infuriate those who have benefited from our gifts and the favor on our lives. It will cause us to become the victim of vicious attacks, (verbal) curses, isolation, and character assassination. We must make sure that we keep ourselves in a position of prayer and fasting during these times, because these attacks have the potential to be so vicious that they can hinder our progression or contaminate our testimonies if we respond to them in an ungodly and fleshly manner. It is during these attacks that we must stand on the promises of Abba and His protection.

When Laban heard that Jacob had left and had taken all of his possessions with him, he was furious and set out intending to harm him when he caught up to him. But before Jacob and Laban had their final confrontation, Abba intervened by visiting Laban in a dream and informing him that Jacob was under His protection, and that no harm was to be done to him. ***(Genesis 31:29)***

When you are obedient and answer the call to "get back to Bethel," God will set a hedge of protection around you. It's extremely important that you understand that the hedge of protection *does not exempt you from experiencing trials and tribulations.*

"Dear brothers and sisters, when troubles of any kind come your way, consider it an opportunity for great joy. For you know that when your faith is tested, your endurance has a chance to grow. So let it grow, for when your endurance is

fully developed, you will be perfect and complete, needing nothing." James 1: 2-4 (NLT)

Because trials and tribulations are needed for our endurance to grow, the hedge of protection *does not* keep us from going through troubles, but it *does* put a limit on how much pressure that the enemy can apply. We know (according to *Isaiah 54:17*) that God will not allow the enemy to "take us out," but He allows the trials and tribulations from the enemy to push us to a point where our endurance can grow strong enough for us to have strength to complete our journey to return to Bethel. Endurance is needed for us to flee Gilead but in addition to endurance, we also have to learn how to stand on the truth of what Abba Father has instructed us to do, as well as what He has done for us. Laban was not going to allow Jacob to simply break ties with him because he understood that Jacob was extremely beneficial to his financial and social status. He knew that everything that he had achieved in the past twenty years was because of the favor on Jacob's life, and he wasn't ready for that to come to an end. Laban was determined to confront Jacob and try to trick him into coming back with him…but Jacob was equally determined to get back to Bethel!

When Laban caught up with Jacob, he was livid. He had every intention of harming him; but because God had warned him against doing so, there was nothing that Laban could do to him except try to use the very thing that had worked on Jacob in the past…trickery and deceit.

The Foundation of Truth

Laban tracked Jacob down in the mountains of Gilead. According to Ellicott's *Commentary for English Readers*, "*The distance from Haran to the most northernly part of this country* was fully three hundred miles. It would require hard riding on the part of Laban and his brethren to enable them to overtake Jacob, even on the borders of this region."

This is exactly what the spirit of religion will do. It does not matter how much distance we put between our past behaviors and associations with the spirit…it will continue to pursue us if it thinks that there is a chance of entangling us again. The only way to sever our ties with the spirit of religion is by using the weapon of truth. We are instructed in the Book of **Ephesians** to *"put on the whole armor of God so that we can stand firm against the wiles of the devil."* A piece of that armor is the Belt of Truth.

Jacob and Laban's relationship is reflective of our association with the spirit of religion. It is a foundation built on trickery and lies, and the only way to dismantle this foundation is with the weapon of truth.

After years of trickery and lies, Laban's final attempt to once more entangle Jacob involved just the right amount of pressure that pushed him to confront his uncle and dismantle the grip he had on his life. Jacob was able to do this by speaking the truth to Laban. Jesus tells us as believers that *"If we abide in Him and are obedient to His word then we are his disciples and that we will not only know the truth but that the truth will make us free." John 8:31-32 (NLT)* The *truth* is what set Jacob free from the trickery and lies of Laban.

In **Genesis 31:36-42**, Jacob lays the *foundation of truth* before his uncle, which revealed the deceitfulness of Laban's actions towards him. Jacob lets his uncle know that he understood that if he (Laban) could have had his way that he would have sent him (Jacob) away empty-handed, but because of the protection of God, Jacob was able to leave with everything that belonged to him. Laban knew that everything Jacob said was true, and there was nothing else for him to do except align himself with the truth. Jacob and his uncle then entered into an agreement to part ways peacefully. They gathered stones and put them in a pile, as a physical marker of their verbal agreement. When we lay the foundation of truth before the enemy, it will cause our enemies to treat us with fairness, even when they are not in agreement with what has taken place.

Boundaries

Laban told Jacob in **Genesis 31:51-52,** *"Look! Here is a pile of stones, and I will never pass them to come after you and you must never pass them to come after me."* These stones not only served as a reminder of their verbal agreement, but also as a physical marker which both Jacob and his uncle agreed never to cross. In the midst of leaving Gilead, we have to learn how to stabilize the rocky places of our spiritual lives by establishing a foundation built on truth and putting in place boundaries which we refuse to cross over.

The enemy knows our likes and dislikes, and he will use whatever tactics necessary to keep us bound, especially if he has been successful with these things in the past. Establishing boundaries in our lives serves as a wall of protection against these tactics and keeps us from becoming entangled in the enemy's grip of trickery and deceit. Jesus tells us in **John 14:26** that *"The Holy Spirit is our teacher and that He will teach us in all things and will remind of everything he has told us."* The Holy Spirit will communicate with us the areas in our lives where we are weak and susceptible to the tactics of the enemy; and when he does, we must then erect boundaries that will protect us from succumbing to or participating in those activities. When we decide that we are no longer willing to go beyond the boundaries which the Holy Spirit led us to erect, then we are on our way to leaving the rough places of Gilead.

It was when Jacob took the oath before the God of his father Isaac to respect the boundary line that Laban finally recognized that Jacob was truly free from his grip, and he understood that there was no longer anything he could do that would keep Jacob under his control. To assure that he could retain that which he had already gained by Jacob's hand, he basically told Jacob, "You don't bother me, and I won't bother you," and Jacob agreed. The next morning, Laban kissed his daughters and grandchildren goodbye and headed home. Jesus tells us in **John 14:6** that ***"I am the way, the truth, and the life. No one can come to the Father except through me."*** Believers, the only way we are going to escape the rugged terrain of Gilead is through the guidance of the Holy Spirit and by establishing boundaries and standing on the foundation of truth.

Time for Reflection…

-Have you felt the Lord calling you to return to Him? Is there a "rocky terrain" that you must cross on your journey?

-In order for Jacob to break free of the strongholds in his life, he had to set boundaries. This was particularly true when it came to his Uncle Laban. Is there someone in your life with whom you either have in the past needed to or need to now, establish boundaries? What are some practices that you have used (or can use) to do this?

- When we hear the call of God tugging at our hearts for us to return to Him, our response should be like Jacob…a response of obedience. Jacob answered the call. Will we?

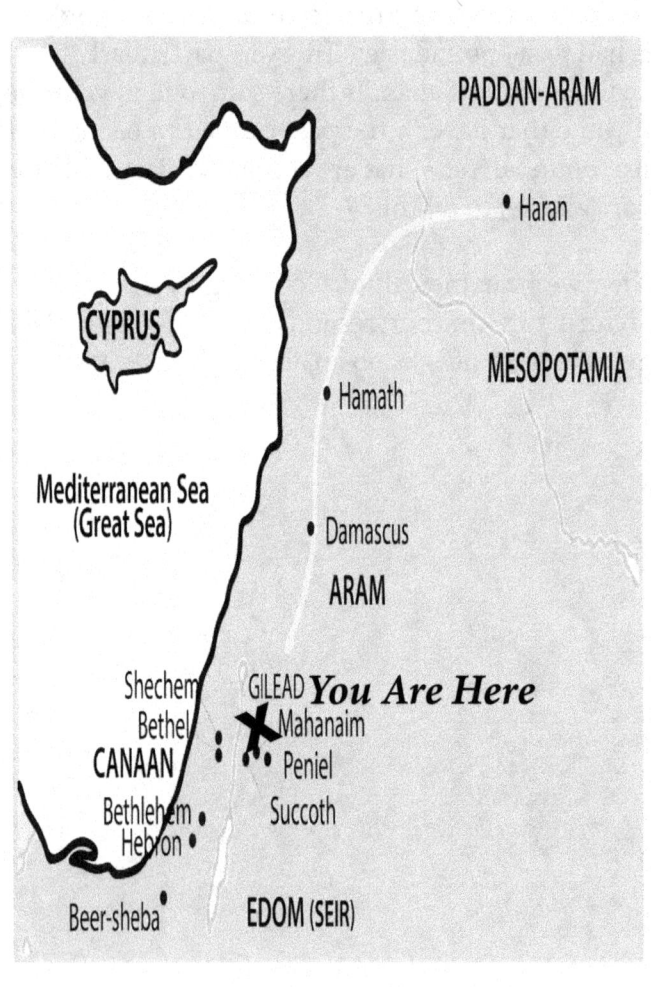

Chapter 3

Mahanaim: Deliverance from Double-Minded Thinking

"Jacob went on his way, and the angels of God met him. And when Jacob saw them he said, 'This is God's camp!' So, he called the name of that place Mahanaim."
Genesis 32: 1-2 (NLT)

Jacob has just had a confrontation with Laban and now finds himself in Mahanaim. God instructed Jacob to return to Bethel, which meant that he had to travel through Mahanaim. It would ultimately be the place where God ordained for him to face his greatest fear and an opportunity for Jacob to cry out to God in a manner which he never had before. At this point in his life, Jacob had been running from his past for the last *twenty years*. His obedience to follow God's calling on his life would now open a door that Jacob had closed when he fled from his brother in fear for his life.

> *Mahanaim represents the place where we can clearly see that God is with us, but we don't really know Him as Abba Father, a Father that watches over His Word to perform it.*

Jacob clearly saw that God was camped in this location along with him, which gave him the strength to send messengers to his brother. But Jacob's courage immediately vanished, and he became greatly distressed and afraid when the messengers returned and told him that Esau was coming to meet him, and that he was riding with 400 men. ***(Genesis 32:3-7)***

The Danger of the Double Mind

Mahanaim is defined as *"two camps."* When we are breaking free from the spirit of religion, Mahanaim represents the place of double mindedness, which is a dangerous place for believers to dwell. **James 1:8** tells us that *"A double minded man is unstable in all his ways,"* meaning that if the enemy can keep us locked down in this location, we will become stagnant and stale to the things of God. *Spiritually, Mahanaim is a place where the enemy takes pleasure in holding the people of God captive, because he knows that if he can keep us trapped between two opinions, then we will not progress in the things of God.*

It is often the location where our faith is confronted by our fears, where our past confronts our future, and where religion confronts relationship. It is a place where Abba calls us to *completely trust Him* to handle the hard and frightening obstacles in our lives. **Proverbs 3:5-6** tells us that we are to **"Trust in the Lord with all our heart and not depend on our own ways, but seek His will in all we do, and then He will show us the path in which we should take."** *(paraphrase mine)*

When we are stuck in Mahanaim, it is always difficult to know what path to take. It is while we are in this place that we must learn how to put our trust in God and know that if He brings us to a difficult or frightening situation in our life, that we can trust Him and know without wavering that He will show us what to do.

Battling Our Goliath

It is when we are in Mahanaim that we learn through facing our fears how to stand flat-footed, just as David did when he battled Goliath, and allow God to reveal himself as Jehovah Tsaba, "The Lord Our Warrior."

"You come to me with a sword, a spear, and a javelin but I come to you in the name of the Lord of hosts (Jehovah Tsaba), the God of the armies of Israel, whom you have taunted."
I Samuel 17:45 (NLT)

Goliath represents the things in our lives that appear to be unbeatable; the things that taunt us and cause us to live in fear. This is what Jacob experienced when he entered Mahanaim. Even with a clear directive from God Himself to return to his family in the land of his fathers **(Genesis 31:3)** and with the visual proof of God's angels greeting him, Jacob was still held captive to the fear of his past. For Jacob, *his past was his Goliath.*

In the midst of transitioning from the spirit of religion to relationship, we have to travel through Mahanaim. The enemy's goal is to keep us in this place because of its barrenness; as long as we are dwelling in Mahanaim we will never be able to fulfill our God-given destinies. Our adversary does not want us to advance in the things of God; **John 10:10** tells us that his job is to **"steal, kill and destroy."**

The enemy's ultimate plan is to steal the promises of God from us, kill our hopes and dreams of becoming who and doing what God has called us to, and destroying our path to eternal life with the Abba, our Father. One of the tactics that he uses to accomplish this is by holding believers captive in Mahanaim, a spiritual state of double mindedness.

The enemy loves nothing more than to keep the children of God teetering between fear and faith: our natural state and our spiritual reality, belief and unbelief, the spirit of religion, and a pure relationship with God. To defeat this mindset, we have to grab hold of **2 Corinthians 10:3-4**, where we are reminded that we walk in the flesh, but we do not war according to the flesh. For the weapons of our warfare are not carnal but mighty in God for pulling down strongholds, casting down arguments and every high thing that exalts itself against the knowledge of God, bringing every thought into captivity of the obedience of Christ. We will never be able to leave Mahanaim until we understand that the enemy's attack on our mind is a spiritual weapon that he uses to keep us in a continual state of teetering about the promises of God.

Walking By Faith

When we are faced with doubt and uncertainty, we often try and figure things out through natural reasoning, which causes us to go straight into panic mode. Panic mode causes us to operate from a state of intense fear, which causes hysteria and irrational behavior. This is what took place with Jacob when his messengers told him that Esau was on his way to meet him with an army of 400 men. The fear of Esau's previous threats resounded deep down in his soul until he forgot about the angels of God being with him, and he went straight into panic mode. This panic caused Jacob to take his entire household and divide it into two camps, which was *an outward sign of his double minded spiritual state.* Jacob became so focused on his brother's threats against his life that he temporarily forgot about the promises of God.

We must keep in mind that at this point in his life, Jacob had not yet developed his faith and trust in God enough to know that *if God gives us a directive to do something, then He has already cleared the path for it to happen.* This is the case for most of us who find ourselves stuck in the spiritual location of Mahanaim. The reason that the enemy leads us to operate from a state of double mindedness is so that we will disregard the promises of God and instead, focus on our fears, our lack of resources, or our comfort level. In order to overcome this, we must learn to operate by faith. ***Hebrews 11:6*** tells us, *"And it* *is impossible to please God without faith. Anyone who wants to come to him must believe that God exists and that he rewards those who sincerely seek him."*

It is in our seeking that our faith is strengthened and our trust is fortified. Jacob's seeking showed up in the form of an earnest prayer…it was in his greatest fear that Jacob cried out to God. Jacob's prayer included three important elements that caused God to move on his behalf and move him out of Mahanaim.

First, *he referenced God as the true and living God, the God of his father and grandfather.* When we come face-to-face with the Goliaths in our lives that cause us to question who God is, then we must learn to stand on the testimonies of others about who God is and what He has done in their lives and know that *if God came through for them, then He will come through for us!* In **Acts 10:34-35**, Apostle Peter tells us, *"I see very clearly that God shows no favoritism. In every nation he accepts those who fear him and do what is right."*

Second, *Jacob reminded God of the promise which He spoke to him* while he was still with his Uncle Laban, recorded in **Isaiah 43:26**: *"Put me in remembrance: let us plead together…"* The reminder is not for *God* but for *us*…and for the enemy who is launching the attack. The reason Abba gives us a prophecy or a promise is to remind us (and the enemy!) that *our destiny is already declared in the heavens*. It gives us hope, so that we will keep trusting and seeking Abba, our Father, knowing that He will bring us to a place of deliverance. It also serves as a warning to the enemy, to let him know that *"I've called them into greatness and I am watching over my Word to perform it."*

Finally, *he admits his fears*, humbling himself before God. When we release our doubt and fear to Abba, our Father, we are really saying, "Look. I don't have what it takes to complete this task. I need you to show me what to do." *James 4:10* tells us to *"Humble ourselves before the Lord and He will lift us up."*

While in Mahanaim, in addition to trusting Abba and seeking His will for our lives, we have to learn how to cry out to God.

> *"In my distress I cried out to the Lord; yes, I prayed to my God for help. He heard me from his sanctuary; my cry to him reached his ears. Then the earth quaked and trembled. The foundations of the mountains shook; they quaked because of his anger. Smoke poured from his nostrils; fierce flames leaped from his mouth. Glowing coals blazed forth from him. He opened the heavens and came down…He shot his arrows and scattered his enemies; great bolts of lightning flashed, and they were confused… He reached down from heaven and rescued me; he drew me out of deep waters. He rescued me from my powerful enemies; from those who hated me and were too strong for me. They attacked me at a moment when I was in distress, but the Lord supported me. He led me to a place of safety; he rescued me because he delights in me."*
> *Psalm 18: 6-9, 14, 16-19 (NLT)*

When the cries of those who are trusting and seeking God's will for their lives reaches the heart of Abba, those cries become a "spiritual 911 call," and our Father Abba becomes angry, and opens Heaven to come rescue us and lead us to a place of safety. Remember that spiritually Mahanaim is a place where the enemy takes pleasure in holding the people of God captive, because he knows that if he can keep us trapped between two opinions then we will not progress in the things of God. If we are ever going to leave this spiritual location, we must learn how to trust God, seek His will, and cry out to Him from a place of humility.

Time for Reflection…

-For many of us, fear is an "automatic reaction" when we are faced with obstacles in our lives. Is this true in your own life? If so, have you learned to manage your fears? What strategies or practices have you found to be helpful?

-James tells us that "a double-minded man is unstable in all his ways." What do you think that he means by this?

-Jacob put God in remembrance of the promise in which He spoke to him. What are some promises that God has spoken concerning you that you are still waiting to see come to pass? Write them down and put God in remembrance of what He has said about you.

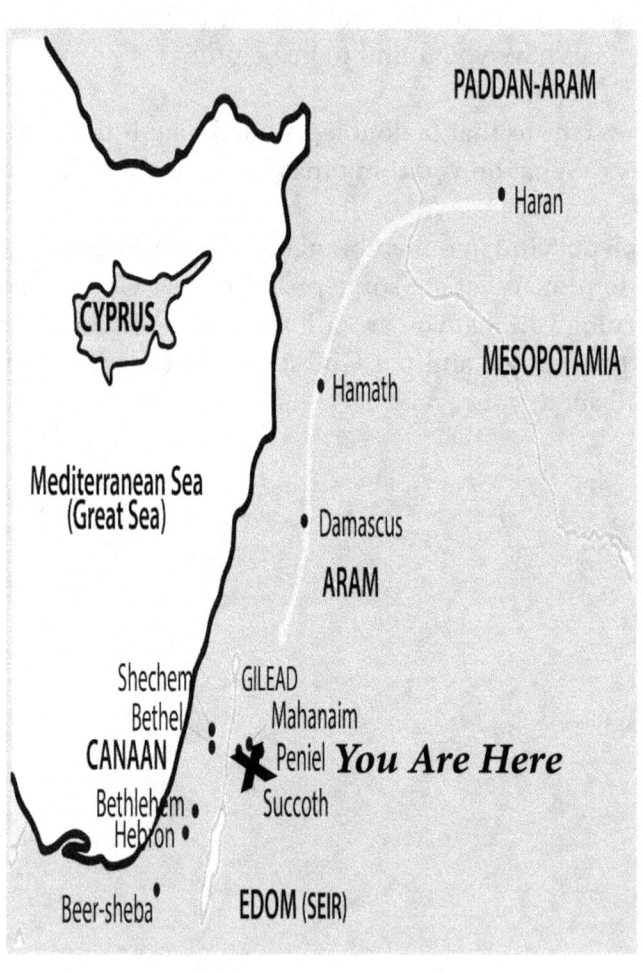

Chapter 4

Peniel:
The Struggle Within

Jacob is in a very desperate state at this point. He is in the process of facing his greatest fear…coming face-to-face with his brother (who he has been running from for the past twenty years) so he cries out to God.

"Head" Knowledge vs. "Heart" Knowledge

Although he cried out to God, Jacob made one mistake before doing so. He formulated his own plan of action. According to **Genesis 32**, Jacob entered Mahanaim and immediately recognized the presence of God. He sent messengers to his brother; and when they returned with the news that his brother was coming to greet him riding with 400 men, Jacob became greatly distressed and divided his entire household into two camps, reasoning with himself that if his brother, Esau, attacked one group, then the other would escape. Jacob allowed fear to pollute his spiritual eyesight. Upon entering the land, he saw the hosts of angels, and he *knew* that God's presence was with him, but he still allowed the spirit of fear to cause him to focus on the natural instead of the supernatural. Our spiritual eyesight becomes polluted when we have *head* knowledge concerning the Word of God and His promises for our lives, but that knowledge has not yet infiltrated our hearts, which means it has not yet translated into *heart* knowledge.

> *Having head knowledge of the promises of God does not translate to having heart knowledge.*

Hebrews 11:1 tells us that *"Faith is the confidence that what we hope for will actually happen; it gives us assurance about things we cannot see." (NLT)* This is what it means to have heart knowledge. Because Jacob's faith was still in "early development," he operated from a place of head knowledge, which caused his spiritual eyesight to be polluted therefore, he was overtaken by fear.

Fear caused Jacob to focus on the "natural" truth which is that his brother, Esau was on his way, and bringing 400 men with him. Jacob knew that his brother was a skillful hunter and warrior, and he assumed that the men riding with him would possess the same skills—so naturally, this was a frightening situation for him.

Because Jacob lacked heart knowledge, the spirit of fear was able to keep him from seeing that God was with him. Heart knowledge keeps us from making the same mistake that Jacob did. It is important that we learn how to "sharpen our spiritual eyesight" so that we have the ability to see beyond the natural into the supernatural; in order to accomplish this, we must "walk by faith and not by sight."

First, We Pray

We see an example of this in the Prophet Elisha praying for his servant. According to *2 Kings 6:15-17,* Elisha's servant woke up one morning and saw troops, chariots, and horses from the enemy surrounding them. He became greatly distressed and asked Prophet Elisha, *"What will we do now?"* Just like Jacob, the servant allowed the spirit of fear to blind him to the supernatural causing him to focus only on the natural, but then Elisha told him not to be afraid because *"There are more on our side than theirs."* Elisha was looking past the natural into the supernatural, and so he prayed to the Lord that his servant's eyes would be opened. When the servant looked up, his spiritual eyes were opened, and he saw that that the hillside around them was filled with horses and chariots of fire.

Jacob made the mistake of not praying to God first, which allowed the spirit of fear to invade his senses and caused him to revert to his old habit of operating in the spirit of religion. We know this because Jacob's initial response to the fact that his brother was on his way was to try and appease him by presenting him with materialistic and fleshly things; this lets us know that the spirit of religion still had a grip on him. But even after Jacob made the move to deceive his brother with smooth words and gifts, and by attempting to secure the safety for his own household by dividing it into two camps, yet he still could not find peace about the matter. He cried out to God in an earnest prayer, and it was this prayer…this cry… that forever changed Jacob's life.

Our first course of action in any situation should be to seek God. In **Philippians 4:6**, we are instructed *"To not worry about anything, but instead pray about it."* We are to tell God what we need, and give Him thanks for it in advance. When we act before we pray, we only add extra stress to the situation. Without praying first, we can never be sure that we have done the right thing, because we don't know the heart or motives of the other individuals that are involved. What we can be assured of is that if we make a mistake and act before we pray, God may not hold that action against us, but acting without praying may cause us to become overly anxious or stressed concerning the situation. But we can be confident in knowing that God will answer when we cry out to Him, and this is what takes place next.

Jacob's prayer caused him to have an encounter with the true and living God. His entire journey thus far had been preparing his heart for this moment with Abba, and without even realizing it, his obedience to God and seeking His will set him up for a face-to-face encounter with the God of his father and grandfather. When we combine obedience to God's command with trusting Him and a humble spirit, it sets us up for a face-to-face encounter with Abba, and this is what happened in Peniel.

Something was taking place inside of Jacob that he had never experienced before. His "spiritual baby," his *destiny*, was ready to come forth. It was such a leaping in his spiritual belly that he could not rest, **Genesis 32:21-24** tells us that Jacob had decided to spend the night in Mahanaim; but during the night, he got up and took his wives and children across the Jabbok River, and then he sent over all his possessions, which left him all alone.

In the Quiet Places

It is in our alone time with God that He deals with the issues of our heart. **Proverbs 23:7** tells us, *"For as one thinks in his heart then so is he,"* and **Proverbs 4:23** tells us to *"Guard our hearts above everything else because it determines the course of our lives."* In order for us to fulfill our God-given destiny, we must be willing to take ourselves to a quiet place and allow God to expose the issues within our hearts.

There will be many situations in our life that cause us to "get up in the middle of the night." When we feel the nudging of the Holy Spirit, we must steal away to a quiet place, so that we can allow God to deal with our heart, our motives, and our ability to trust Him completely. This is what Jacob did.

Jacob was now alone. He had sent his family over the brook, and the "birthing process" was beginning. First, a man came and wrestled with him. We know that this was not "just" a man, because **Hosea 12:4** tells us that it was an angel that came to Jacob. In **Genesis 32:26**, the angel tells Jacob to let him go because the day is breaking. We know that this must have been an intense wrestling match, because they have wrestled all night and now it's going into the next day, and Jacob is still holding on to the angel.

> *Elder Trell James tells us, "We must understand that Jacob was used to wrestling. It was something he had done his entire life. His very first wrestling match was in his mother's womb, against his brother, Esau. He continued to wrestle with him up until the time he left his father's house. He wrestled with his father, and he wrestled with his Uncle Laban—wrestling was nothing new for Jacob. But this wrestling match was different because it wasn't about obtaining material possessions or an earthly title, but rather dealing with the issues of Jacob's heart."*

What Is Your Name?

Our heart is the "central command station" for all of our being and actions. It is our heart that dictates to our mind how we will respond to situations that we face. It is our heart that tells us who we should trust or not trust. It is in the process of birthing our destiny that Abba allows us to look at our own heart. This is why when Jacob told the angel, "I will not let you go until you bless me," the angel asked him, "What is your name?" What the angel was really doing was asking Jacob to look deep within himself and examine his reason for processing and reacting to situations in the manner that he did. What the angel was saying was, *"How do you see yourself?"*

The reason the wrestling match lasted so long was because Jacob had to look deep inside of himself to see his own heart. This was a difficult task for him, because he had to spiritually look behind every wall that he had placed around his own heart due to deceitful interactions with family and friends. For Jacob, these were walls of defense and protection, but to Abba, our Father, they were walls of separation.

Come Out From Behind the Walls

These walls of separation keep us from moving forward into our destiny, because they keep us from fully placing ourselves in the hand of Abba. The walls do not keep us from getting to Abba, but they do keep Him from getting to us. We have the ability to scale these walls to get to Abba when we need Him. When we are in need and cry out an earnest prayer, God is able to come to our rescue, because we have "come from behind the wall." Unfortunately, when we get what we want from Him, we retreat behind the wall again.

It is through the erecting of these walls that the spirit of religion can hold believers in a place of deception, by having us fall back from encountering a true relationship with Abba. This is what we see taking place with the church of Laodicea in the Book of Revelation.

The church of Laodicea was a group of people who were still wrestling with the angel and refusing to look deep within themselves. The angel of the church revealed that this was keeping them from fulfilling their God-given destinies. He told them that they were neither hot nor cold, **"But since you** *are like lukewarm water, neither hot nor cold, I will spit you out of my mouth."* **Revelation 3:16 (NLT)** They were just like Jacob in many respects: they were financially stable, and they knew enough about God not to deny Him, yet they refused to remove the walls from around their hearts so that Abba could have total access.

> *Walls of separation are erected on the foundation of free will, which means that God Himself will not remove them...this is something we must do.*

Jesus told them in **Revelation 3:20,** *"Listen! I stand at the door and knock; if anyone hears my voice and opens the door, I will come into their house and eat with them and they will eat with me."* **(NLT)**

Open My Eyes

Jacob heard the angel that night and he opened the door. He decided that he wanted his God-given destiny more than anything that he had achieved as "Jacob." The wrestling throughout the night had not only removed the walls and opened the door, but it also sharpened Jacob's "spiritual eyesight." He was now able to see himself in his current spiritual state: Jacob, the "heel grabber;" the one who obtained things through crafty and deceitful measures. The process of looking beyond our materialistic possessions and earthly titles to see ourselves as we truly are without pretense or through the perception of what or who others deemed us to be is an extremely intense battle that can only be accomplished with acute spiritual eyesight.

The writer of **Psalm 119:18** asked the Lord to *"Open my eyes so that I may see the wonderful truths in your instruction,"* and this is what takes place with Jacob when he told the angel, *"I will not let you go until you bless me."* Jacob had material wealth and earthly titles, but he wanted more. He wanted to become who God had created him to be. He knew that to accomplish this, his spiritual eyesight had to be extremely keen, so that he could bypass what he saw in the natural and operate in full obedience to the wonderful truths of Abba's instructions.

> *"Your name will no longer be Jacob, from now on you will be called Israel because you have fought with God and with men and you have won. 'Please tell me your name,' Jacob said. 'Why do you want to know my name?' Then he blessed Jacob there and Jacob named the place Peniel (which means 'face of God'), for he said, 'I have seen God face-to-face, yet my life has been spared.'"*
> Genesis 32:28-30 (NLT)

A change had taken place. The wrestling match allowed the walls around Jacob's heart to be removed. Jacob was able to look inside himself and acknowledge the truth about the deceptive nature of who he had been his entire life. His spiritual eyes were opened, and he was able to see the wonderful truth of who God had created him to be: **"Israel. The one who fights with God and wins."**

The Birthing Room

The wrestling match is the battleground to which God calls us, so that we can see the hard truths about ourselves. It is during the wrestling, the "birthing process," that we have to face who we *are*, what we *feel*, and who we are willing to *become*.

The birthing room is a messy place to be. It is the point where we feel the most excruciating pain that we have ever felt in our lives; yet, it is an important place. This is the place where we see God face-to-face, and we have to decide whether or not we are willing to surrender what we have obtained and who we have become, into His hands, so that our true purpose can come forth. *Jeremiah 18* tells us that *"We are the clay and Abba is the potter,"* and when He sees that we are spoiled, that our spiritual eyesight is dull, then He can make us over until we are pleasing to Him, so that we are able to believe the wonderful truths about who He has created us to be. Part of becoming who God had created Jacob to be included making amends with his brother, Esau, and repenting for his previous actions. Jacob was only able to do this *after* he had wrestled with God.

The beginning of **Genesis 33** shows us that a change had taken placed in Jacob's heart. Before his wrestling match with the angel, Jacob had the audacity to try and appease his brother by "paying him off." But now, since wrestling with God and "owning" who he had been in the past, we see a visible change in Jacob.

> *"Jacob looked up and saw Esau coming with his 400 men. So he divided the children among Leah, Rachel and his two servant wives. He put the servant wives and their children in the front, Leah and her children next, and Rachel and Joseph last. Then Jacob went on ahead. As he approached his brother, he bowed to the ground seven times before him. Then Esau ran to meet him and embraced him, threw his arms around his neck, and kissed him.*
> *And they both wept."*
> *Genesis 33:1-3 (NLT)*

The Ministry of Reconciliation

Jacob's actions described here are a part of the ministry of reconciliation (which we are all called to be a part of) in action.

"This means that anyone who belongs to Christ has become a new person. The old life is gone; a new life has begun! And all of this is a gift from God, who brought us back to himself through Christ. And God has given us this task of reconciling people to him"
2 Corinthians 5:17- 18 (NLT)

We see that Jacob is now walking in the confidence of what he sees with new, spiritual eyes. He now understands that he has a command to get back to Bethel, and that nothing and no one can stop it. Because he has acknowledged the nature of the old man, Jacob knows he must now show others (especially his brother) that he is no longer Jacob, but Israel, and because he is now walking as Israel, he understands that there is an assignment attached to his life; a God-given destiny that he must fulfill. Part of that is reconciling with his brother, Esau, in a manner that brings glory to Abba, his Father.

Jacob accomplishes this by putting himself in front of all his earthly treasures and bowing down before his brother seven times, which represented total submission. His acts of repentance were accepted by Esau, and they embraced each other and wept. Jacob's obedience, his humble submission and crying out to God, and his willingness to wrestle with the angel until God blessed him has all been acknowledged in this embrace of reconciliation between two brothers that had been separated for over twenty years.

The key to unlocking our God-given destiny involves the *ministry of reconciliation*. We first must be reconciled to Abba, our Father, through repentance and accepting the work of Christ on the cross. After we have done this, we must come to the understanding that we are called to be ambassadors for Christ, meaning that our words and actions should be presented to others in a manner that creates a hunger for them to experience the presence of Abba, our Father, for themselves.

This is what Prophetess Sophia Ruffin's ministry did for me. It created a hunger in me to see the hand of God operate in my life in the same manner that He did in hers, not so that I could obtain the exact same things that Prophetess Ruffin has, but so that I could walk out my God-given destiny and purpose. The only way that this could be accomplished was by wrestling with God and coming to know my true identity through the eyes of Abba, our Father.

"I will take you from every nation and country and bring you back to your own land. I will sprinkle clean water on you and make you clean from all your idols and everything else that has defiled you. I will give you a new heart and a new mind. I will take away your stubborn heart of stone and give you an obedient heart. I will put my spirit in you and will see to it that you follow my laws and keep all the commands I have given you. Then you will live in the land I gave your ancestors. You will be my people and I will be your God." Ezekiel 36:24-28 (NLT)

Wrestling and Repentance

It is in the wrestling that we are called to repent and turn from our former ways. We are then filled with the Holy Spirit, so that we can move closer to our God-given destiny and dwell with Him in Bethel.

Getting Back to Bethel

Due to his determination to be blessed, Jacob was left with a lifelong limp, which meant that he no longer walked like he did before his wrestling match. We must be willing to wrestle with God, to the point that others will be able to see a spiritual change in us that will produce a hunger for them to walk with Abba in the same manner. Paul urges us as believers in **Colossians 1:10** to *"Walk in a manner worthy of the Lord,"* meaning that everything that we do should be done so that it not only pleases Him and brings honor to Him, but so that it also draws others to Him.

Walking in a manner that is worthy of the Lord requires us to walk through Peniel, where we are going to have to endure the process of wrestling with the angel of the Lord until it brings us to the point of total surrender. It is in this place that we surrender who we have become through the mishandling of others, our life circumstances, and through our own choices. It is the place of divine exchange where we change the old for the new, the weak for the strong, and the timid for the bold. It is the place where our spiritual eyesight is so keen that we are no longer moved by our natural circumstances. We now possess the ability to set our gaze into the supernatural realm, where we can hear and see the wonderous plan that Abba has for our life. And because of this divine exchange, we are able to reach Bethel and fulfill our God-given destiny.

Time for Reflection...

-"It is in our alone time with God that He deals with the issues of our heart." Do you believe that this is true? Do you make it a practice to have regular, uninterrupted time alone with God? If so, do you find that He "deals with the issues of your heart" during this time? Why or why not?

-After Jacob wrestled with the angel, he was left with a limp—a physical reminder of his struggle with the Lord. A limp can also be spiritual. Have you struggled with the Lord and found that you have been left with a "spiritual limp" that causes others to notice that there is something different about you?

-The angel asked Jacob, "What is your name?" Do you understand the significance of this? Have you ever answered this question yourself? If so... *What is your name?*

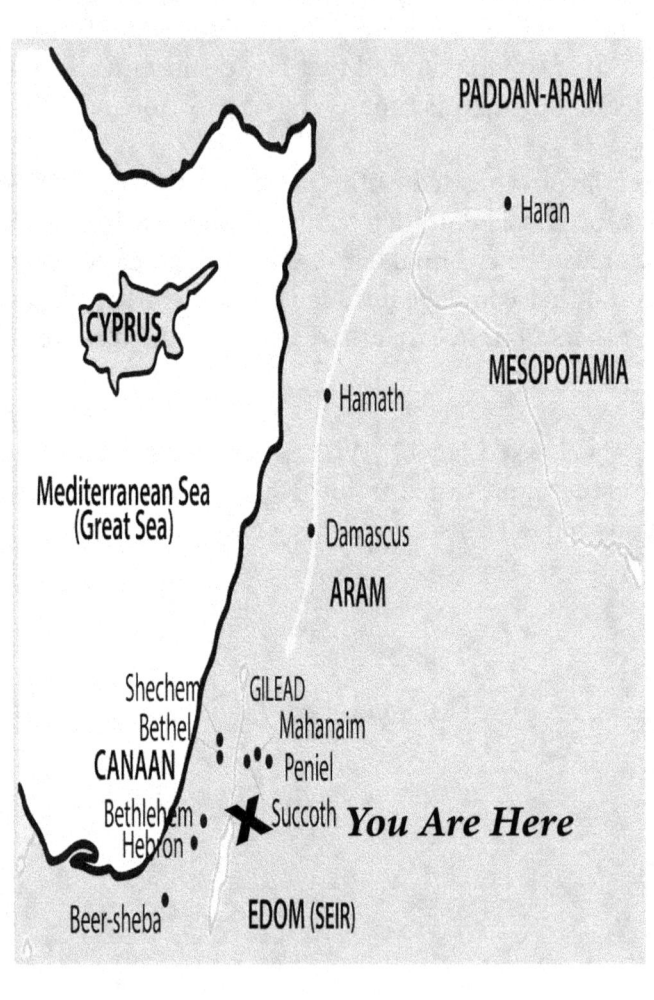

Chapter 5

Succoth:
Under the Shelter of His Wings

The reason Jacob had to flee his father's house was due to his own deceitful actions. He "bought" his brother's birthright from him for a bowl of soup, and he schemed with his mother to trick his father into bestowing upon him the blessing that belonged to Esau. For Esau, Jacob stealing his blessing was the final straw. He had had enough of his brother's scheming ways and vowed to kill him. Now, after twenty years of running from his brother, Jacob had come full circle, and was ready to make amends for his actions. He was finally at a point in his life where he was willing to let go of his old nature as Jacob and walk into his God-given destiny as Israel.

In the reunion between Jacob and his brother, we see Israel starting to emerge as Jacob approaches his brother. Jacob greets Esau first and humbly bows before him seven times as a sign of total submission. Humility is necessary if we are to move from operating in the spirit of religion, to dwelling in Bethel. Jesus told the disciples in *Matthew 18:3-4*: *"I tell you the truth, unless you turn from your sins and become like little children, you will never get into the Kingdom of Heaven. So, anyone who becomes as humble as this little child is the greatest in the Kingdom of Heaven."*

A Humble and Repentant Heart

When Jacob bowed down to Esau, he was not showing humility to Esau out of fear, but rather it was an *outward mani-*

festation of the transformation that had taken place on the inside. Jacob bowing to his brother revealed a repentant heart and humble submission to Abba, our Father.

Psalm 51:17 tells us that God requires us to offer up a humble spirit as a sacrifice, and that He will not reject a humble and repentant heart. Although Jacob was now spiritually walking in his God-given authority as Israel, he had not yet learned how to put his body and soul completely under subjection to his spirit. The Apostle Paul instructs the believers on the importance of living after the spirit and not the flesh in **Romans 8**. Verses 12 and 13 remind us that we have no obligation to do what our sinful nature urges us to do, and if we live by its dictates we will die; but if we learn how to put to death the deeds of our sinful nature, we will live. Sinful nature is often thought of as lust, fornication, adultery, lying etc., but whenever we are disobedient to the voice of God in our lives, it is our sinful nature that is in control.

> *Now may the God of peace make you holy*
> *in every way and may your whole spirit*
> *and soul and body be kept blameless*
> *until our Lord Jesus Christ comes again."*
> *I Thessalonians 5:23 (NLT)*

Created in the Image of God

Genesis 1:27 tells us that we are created in the image of God, and because we serve a triune God, we are comprised of three parts: spirit, soul, and body. The physical makeup of mankind is the body, which consists of our ability to see, feel, taste, smell, and hear. Our soul is made up of our mind, emotions, and will. Our spirit is the breath of God. **Genesis 2:7** tells us that when God formed man from the dust of the ground, *it was only after the breath of God that he became alive.* It is our spirit that connects us to the heart of God, and until we accept

Jesus Christ, we remain spiritually dead. The only way that we can be made alive again is by accepting Jesus Christ as our Lord and Savior and inviting the Holy Spirit to come dwell inside of us. *Ephesians 1:13* says that it is through Jesus that we have heard the Word of Truth and the gospel of salvation, and when we believe in Him, He stamps us with ownership by giving us the Holy Spirit. It is the Holy Spirit that helps our spirit keep our sinful nature under submission.

If we are going to ever leave Succoth, we must learn how to put ourselves under the authority of the Holy Spirit by staying in constant communication with Abba, our Father. Jacob did not do this, but instead, he allowed his own desires and his sinful nature to override his spirit, and he lied to his brother. *Genesis 33:12-17* captures the exchange between Jacob and Esau.

> *"Esau said, 'Let's be going. I will lead the way.' But Jacob replied, 'You can see, my lord, that some of the children are very young, and the flocks and herds have their young, too. If they are driven too hard, even for one day, all the animals could die. Please, my lord, go ahead of your servant. We will follow slowly, at a pace that is comfortable for the livestock and the children. I will meet you at Seir.' 'Alright,' Esau said, 'But at least let me assign some of my men to guide and protect you.' Jacob responded, 'That's not necessary. It's enough that you've received me warmly, my lord!' So Esau turned around and started back to Seir that same day. Jacob, on the other hand, traveled on to Succoth..." (NLT)*

Spiritual Warfare

Jacob told his brother that he would meet him in Seir, but he didn't. He not only turned and went in the opposite direction, but he also built a house for himself and shelters for his herds in a place he called "Succoth," which means "shelters."

Getting Back to Bethel

I firmly believe that Jacob had every intention of traveling to Seir, but after Esau left his presence, Jacob realized just how exhausted he was. He had been engaged in intense spiritual warfare ever since he decided to be obedient to the call of God on his life. He had packed up his wives, children, servants, and herds, and fled from his uncle's house. He then had to endure an intense confrontation with his Uncle Laban, wrestle with God to the point of surrender, and, after twenty years of running for his life from Esau…Jacob finally had to face him. At this point, I believe that Jacob is simply exhausted, and he reacted like many of us who are entangled in the spirit of religion have done. He took a deep breath of relief because the battle was over, and he retreated to his man-made shelter.

Jacob had just been through some intense spiritual warfare and he was also in the beginning stages of forming a relationship with Abba, our Father. He was hearing His voice, he knew he was surrounded by angels, and he had just wrestled with an angel who blessed him with the wonderful instructions of Abba for his life. The mistake that Jacob made was that he *forgot to take the experiences with him as he continued on his journey.* I believe that he was so caught up in winning the battles that he forgot to walk in the assurance of who Abba proved to be through his victorious circumstances.

The Mountaintop

> District Missionary Brenda James of the Gainesville District tells us that we must "remember to bring the mountaintop experience down with us." This means that whenever we encounter the presence of God in the manner that the disciples did during the transfiguration of Jesus on the High Mount in Matthew 17, we should not be so eager to build physical shelters where we will leave the experience on the mountaintop; but we should instead build spiritual shelters, so that we can burn that encounter into our spiritual being as a testimony to the power of our God.

This is what Jacob should have done with his mountaintop experiences.

- When he was confronted by his Uncle Laban and Abba protected him.
- When he entered Mahanaim—the place where he saw the camp of angels.
- When he wrestled with the angel of God and was blessed for doing so.
- When he received the favor that Abba showed him during his reunion with his brother, Esau.

Jacob *should* have built spiritual shelters with those mountaintop experiences and kept communing with Abba—but he *didn't*, and this caused him to attempt to make a permanent dwelling place in a location that was only supposed to be temporary.

Because Jacob did not keep the lines of communication open with God, it delayed his return to Bethel for several years. Delay is what the enemy wants us to experience while we are in Succoth. *I Peter 5:8* warns us to *"Stay alert! Watch out for your great enemy, the devil. He prowls around like a roaring lion, looking for someone to devour."*

We become an easy prey for the enemy when we retreat to our man-made shelters and cease to communicate with Abba, our Father. One of the greatest traps that the enemy sets for us while we are in Succoth is getting us to build physical shelters by participating in mindless behaviors such as withdrawing to the television, Facebook, video games, sleeping, etc. Resting through the process of retreating is not a terrible thing but there is a proper way in which we are to retreat, and Prophet Elijah shows us how to do it.

During the time that he was dwelling in the shelter under the broom tree and in the cave, Elijah remained in constant fellowship with Abba. Not only did he listen to God, but he was extremely honest with what was going through his mind and the exhaustion that he was feeling in his body. Elijah understood that the retreat was necessary for him to get much-needed rest for the remainder of his journey, and he remembered to take experiences of his past victories into his place of retreat.

There is *nothing wrong* with retreating and resting. Jesus beckons us to rest in **Matthew 11:28-29**: *"...come to me, all of you who are weary and carry heavy burdens, and I will give you rest. Take my yoke upon you. Let me teach you because I am humble and gentle at heart and you will find rest for your souls."* Abba, our Father, understands that we are going to get tired, but when we do, we are to rest *in* Him and *not* away from Him. We should find comfort from dwelling in the shelter that He builds for us and not those that we build ourselves.

Time for Reflection…

-When we think of "shelter," we usually think of a place of safety. "Shelters" can also be "walls" though designed to keep us away from whatever it is that we don't want to face. These can take many forms and can be physical, such as retreating behind TVs, video games, or even a book. Anything designed to "keep the world out" can be a wall. They can also be non-physical. Emotional "shelters" or "walls," can be highly effective at keeping people out of our hearts and minds. Do you have "shelters" that you have set up to keep people (including God!) at arm's length? Are they physical or emotional?

-Have you ever had a "mountaintop" experience? Where were you? Were there others with you, and if so, did they have the same experience? How has that experience affected your walk with the Lord?

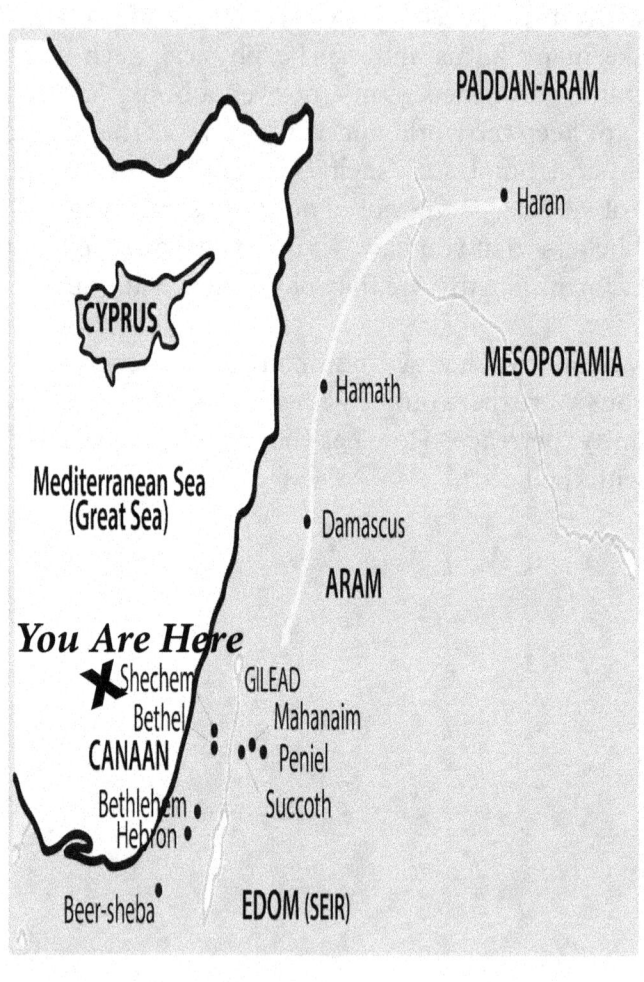

Chapter 6

Shechem: Journey Out of the Comfortable Places

Jacob decides to leave Succoth, but instead of traveling on to Bethel as God had directed him to, he chose to settle in Shechem. Shechem seemed like a great place for Jacob to purchase some land and settle down with his family and possessions. The only problem is that this is not the place where God ordained for him to be. According to Bible.org, Shechem was about thirty miles away from Bethel.

The Substitute Blessing

It seems unimaginable that Jacob would get so close to fulfilling his God-given destiny of getting back to Bethel and not follow it through, but instead, settle for something less than the promise. As long as we are operating in the spirit of religion, we can never obtain the promises of God; and because the enemy understands this, he uses it to his advantage. The enemy knows that our spiritual longing to fulfill our God-ordained destiny never goes away…that is until we are completely walking in our purpose. So, what he attempts to do is gratify our desire by presenting us with a substitute for what God has for us.

When we examine the substitute from the outside, it seems like a good thing. It is only when we partake of it that we realize that although it started out being a good thing, the ultimate purpose and plan of the enemy was to inflict pain, destruction, and death. This is exactly what happened to Eve in the Garden of Eden. *Genesis 3:6* tells us that *"...she saw that the tree was beautiful and its fruit looked delicious, and she wanted the wisdom it would give her. So, she took some of the fruit and ate it. Then she gave some to her husband, who was with her, and he ate it too."*

Eve's decision to partake in eating of the fruit was the cause of her spiritual death, which is to be separated from Abba, our Father. To Jacob, Shechem seemed like a good place. It was large enough to hold all of his herds, had perfect grazing land, and was located just outside of the city; so technically, he wasn't "dwelling" with the people of Shechem. Shechem was so pleasing to Jacob that he built an altar there and named it El-Elohe-Israel which means *"God! The God of Israel."* Jacob was so sure that God would dwell with him in Shechem that he "honored" Him with an altar and acknowledged Him as the God of Israel. Jacob knew in his heart that this was not the place that God was calling him to, so he attempted to appease Abba by acknowledging him as his God.

The Altar of Superficial Sacrifice

This is the same thing that we do when we are operating in the spirit of religion. We attempt to gain Abba's approval in our acts of disobedience. However, His approval and satisfaction cannot be gained by building altars and offering up superficial sacrifices. *I Samuel 15:22* tells us that *"Obedience is better than sacrifices."* We build up altars under the spirit of religion by continuing to take part in things that are not pleasing to Abba, such as those outlined in *Galatians 5:19-21*, including *"...sexual immorality, impurity, lustful pleasures, idolatry, sorcery, hostility, quarreling, jealousy, outbursts of anger, selfish ambition, dissension, division, envy, drunkenness, wild parties and other sins like these."*

Then we try to appease Him by continuing to participate in church ministries and events such as singing in the choir or on the praise team, attending every church function or conference that we can, and giving our offerings and tithes, not realizing that our deeds are tainted because we are still active participants in things that Abba has not ordained as part of our destiny. **Proverbs 14:12** warns us that *"There is a way that seems right to many, but in the end, it leads to death."* Jacob made the decision to accept the substitute that the enemy presented to him and settled in Shechem. He did this because it seemed like a good choice for him but in the end, it was filled with pain, destruction, and death.

> *Abba never designed pain, destruction, and death to be a part of our destiny!*

A Roaring Lion

The Bible tells us that everything God created was *good*. We have to understand that although Abba will use the pain and destruction of life to propel us toward our destiny, *He never instituted it as a requirement for us to walk into our God-ordained destinies.* Jacob's decision to settle in a place that Abba never called him to ended up causing great pain and destruction for his family. His daughter endured a horrific act of violence, which caused her brothers to defend her honor by retaliating with a vicious plan of slaughter for all the males in the city of Shechem.

The enemy's ultimate plan is to keep us from dwelling in the presence of Abba for eternity, so what he does is try to hinder us from getting into Abba's presence while we are living, hoping that we will miss the opportunity to spend eternity in His presence.

I Peter 5:8 tells us to stay alert because *"Our enemy the Devil roams around like a roaring lion, looking for someone to devour."* The fact that Peter uses the description of the lion in this passage to describe our enemy clues us in to the tactics that he uses. A lion will lie in wait for the opportune time to attack. That is why the enemy will offer us substitutes such as Shechem, that are pleasing to our eyes, because his goal is for us to become lethargic to the things of God. He understands that it is in our state of lethargy that we will lose focus on our God-ordained destiny.

Shechem looked like a good place for Jacob to dwell but the enemy was lying in wait for the moment in which Jacob became inattentive to his surroundings. When he did, he launched an attack that was intended to cause Jacob so much pain and turmoil that he would ultimately give up and walk away from the promises of God.

The Danger of Being Comfortable

The danger of remaining in Shechem is that it is a place where we can easily become comfortable. It is a place that is designed to lure us into a state of inattentiveness, because it is in this state that we are most vulnerable to the attacks of the enemy. And if by chance the attack is not vicious enough to kill us immediately, then he will use it to launch a slow kill attack that includes the spirit of division, shame, and guilt, which is a doorway for other spiritual attacks to enter in, ultimately resulting in a slow spiritual death.

We see this taking place in the conversation that Jacob had with his sons after their retaliation on the men of Shechem. In *Genesis 34:30,* Jacob tells his sons Simeon and Levi, *"You have ruined me! You've made me stink among all the people of this land—among all the Canaanites and Perizzites. We are so few that they will join forces and crush us. I will be ruined, and my entire household will be wiped out!"*

When we are dwelling in Shechem and things go sideways, we often fail to take responsibility for our part in the destruction and pain that was brought our way. Instead, we blame others for "messing up our good thing." We clearly see the spirit of division in operation, because Jacob's response is "all about him." He is afraid that *he* will be "ruined and made to stink," and that "all *he* had will be crushed." He fails to see that it was *his choice* to be disobedient to the calling of God that brought the pain, destruction, and death that his *family* was now dealing with.

The Prodigal Son

Although the enemy's plan is to use pain, destruction, and death to destroy us, Abba uses it to restore us back to our God-ordained destiny. We see this in action when Jesus tells us about the parable of the Prodigal Son in **Luke 15**. In this parable, a man's youngest son sees a distant land that is more pleasing to him than his father's home. He requests his portion of his inheritance and strikes out on his own, only to find himself soon living with the pigs. It is only after he has left his father's home and endured hardship and pain that he realizes this is not the good place he thought it was and makes the decision to return to his father's house. On his way home, the father sees him returning from far off and is filled with so much love and compassion that he runs to him. The son then repents of his actions, and the father in return welcomes him home and restores him to his rightful position.

The love and compassion that the father has for his son in this parable is the same love that Abba had for Jacob, and that He has for us. *Isaiah 54:17* tells us that *"No weapon formed against us may prosper,"* which means that the enemy's plan of destruction for us in Shechem may be a painful experience that leaves us wounded...*but it will not destroy us.* We know from **Genesis 50:20** that God will take that which the enemy meant for harm and use it for His good.

Our decision to dwell in Shechem may cause us some delays as well as some pain and destruction, but it will not destroy us. We must understand that this is not the place that Abba has ordained for us to die. Even in our disobedience to God, He remains faithful to us. **Jeremiah 31:3** tells us that Abba has always loved us with an everlasting love and therefore has called us with loving kindness, meaning that His love for us encompasses so much tenderness and compassion that our actions cannot deter His love or the calling He has on our lives, *as long as we are willing to continue seeking after the things of God.*

Romans 8:1-2 reminds us, **"Now there is no condemnation for those of us who belong to Christ Jesus, and it is because we belong to him that the power of life that is given through him has freed us from the power of sin and death."** There is no need for us to continue to dwell in a place that brings so much pain, devastation, and death. This is not the expected end that Abba has for us...He is waiting for us to arrive at our God-ordained destiny which is Bethel! In **Genesis 35:1**, He tells Jacob to go to Bethel at once and live there...and He is saying the same thing to us. All that is required of us is to repent of our disobedience and continue on our journey of getting to Bethel...the place where God dwells.

Time for Reflection…

-Shechem is our "spiritual comfort zone." It's the place where we feel pretty good about where we are in life. And it is easy to rationalize that if *we* feel good about where we are, then *God* must feel good about where we are. What is the danger in doing this? How can we break out of our spiritual comfort zone and finish the race that has been laid out before us?

-It has been said that "God doesn't waste pain." In the case of the Prodigal Son, he had to go through the experience in order to fully understand the love that his father had for him. Can you think of a painful time in your life that the Lord has redeemed? What did that redemption look like?

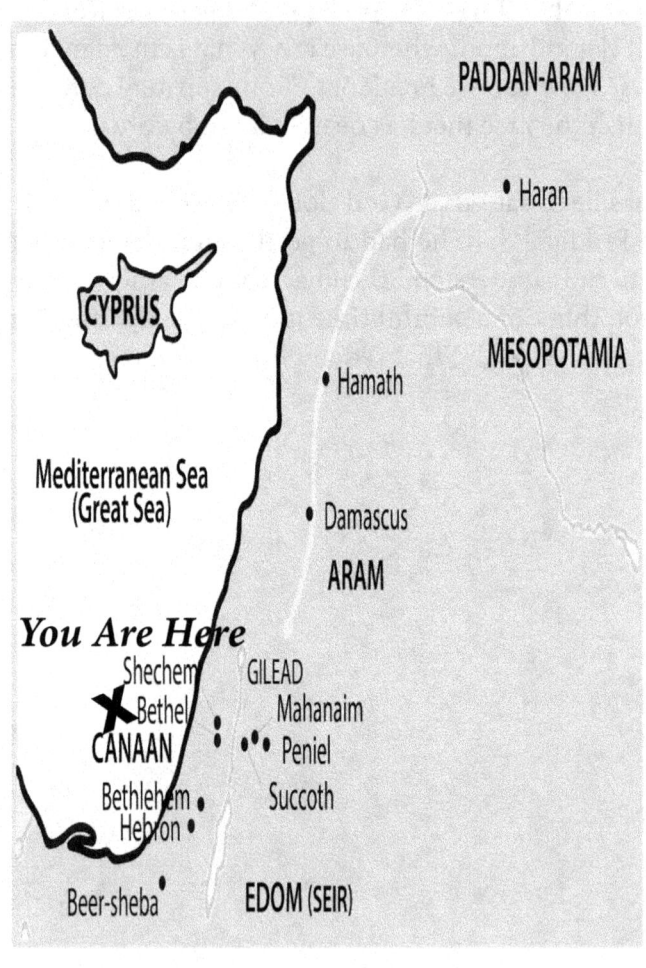

Chapter 7

Bethel: Returning to Our God

"Then God said to Jacob, 'Get ready and move to Bethel and settle there. Build an altar there to the God who appeared to you when you fled from your brother, Esau.'"
Genesis 35:1 (NLT)

God is now calling Jacob back to the place where he first encountered Him. The place where Jacob was so in awe of his encounter with Abba that he named the place *"House of God."* Jacob responds to the call, and in pure obedience, he instructs his family to get rid of all their pagan idols, purify themselves, and change their garments because they are going to Bethel, to dwell with the God who has been with him wherever he has gone.

The Courage to Stand

While on his journey, a lot was revealed to Jacob— both about himself and about the God whom he vowed to worship. Jacob gained the courage to stand up for himself, and he overcame some of his greatest fears. He came to understand his human characteristics, he endured some devasting hardships that forever changed the dynamics of his family, and he also learned some wonderful truths about the plans that Abba had for him.

Jacob also came to know Abba in a very intimate way, although throughout his journey, it didn't seem like an intimate connection was being formed between him and Abba. Jacob's journey through Haran, Gilead, Mahanaim, Peniel, Succoth, and Shechem brought him closer to the God of his father and grandfather, by revealing to him the characteristics of the God that he had vowed to serve.

Jacob learned the importance of *talking with, listening to, trusting in,* and *obeying* God. His journey brought him to the realization that the God who introduced himself to him as **"The LORD, the God of your grandfather Abraham, and the God of your father Isaac," (Genesis 28:13 NLT)** had now became the God of Jacob.

As it was for Jacob, so it is for us; our journey back to Bethel through the places of Haran, Gilead, Mahanaim, Peniel, Succoth, and Shechem is designed to bring us into an intimate communion with Abba that cannot be forfeited or tainted.

No Hidden Agendas

Intimacy with Abba is formed throughout the journey of our lives. Every experience that we encounter while journeying back to Bethel is designed to bring us to a place of fellowship that we have never tapped into before. It is intimacy that requires us to stand before Him with no hidden agendas other than to be in His presence. It is the same type of intimacy that God had with Adam and Eve before they disobeyed Him in the Garden of Eden. **Genesis 2:25** reminds us that *"The man and his wife were both naked, but they felt no shame."*

This is the significance of Jacob instructing his family to get rid of the idols, clean themselves, and change their garments. The changing of the garments, getting rid of the idols and purging themselves was an outward sign of the spiritual cleansing that was taking place on the inside of Jacob. Jacob understood that Bethel is a Holy and intimate place, and that if he was going to dwell there, then he had to present himself Holy unto God. For this reason, Jacob and his family purified themselves so that they could stand spiritually naked before Abba.

James 1:2-4 gives a perfect explanation of how this intimacy is formed, and why it is necessary. **"Dear brothers and sisters, when troubles come your way, consider it an opportunity for great joy. For you know that when your faith is tested, your endurance has a chance to grow. So, let it grow, for when your endurance is fully developed, you will be perfect and complete needing nothing."**

In these Scriptures, James reminds us that when we encounter troubled times, we should consider it a time of great joy because there is a spiritual transformation that is taking place in the midst of the trouble. He also gives us the necessary nugget we need to overcome; he tells us that the only reason that we are going through this trial is because it is a testing of our faith, and it is through trials and tribulations that our faith in Abba grows, and we become more intimate with Him. It is during this process that we develop the endurance that we need to complete the journey into Bethel.

The Narrow Door of Faith

Bethel is a very intimate place that can only be accessed by going through the narrow door of faith in Abba and only Abba. In order to gain access through the door of faith, we must trust completely in God, His Word, and His promises. We cannot depend on our own abilities or the abilities of others, but we must operate fully in the principle of *Proverbs 3:5*, not depending on our natural abilities but trusting in Him with all our hearts, seeking His will in everything that we do, and walking the path that He shows us. By doing this, we are able to dwell in Bethel and we will be complete, needing nothing, which produces freedom from the spirit of religion.

There is a freedom that comes with dwelling in Bethel because we know that this is the place where Abba is, and there is no room for worry, fear, or doubt because we are in the presence of our all-knowing, all-powerful-Father. This freedom is not possible when we are trapped in the spirit of religion, because it keeps us from realizing that continually dwelling in Abba's presence is a possibility. So instead of seeking for the dwelling place of Abba, we become satisfied with "momentary encounters" in His presence. By becoming intimate with Abba, we open ourselves up to the purest form of communication, which is built on a foundation of freedom, worship, obedience, and trust.

The Importance of Communication

Even though Jacob's first encounter with Abba was a very intimate and personal experience, he didn't carry the experience with him, but instead left it at the place where he made his vow. He didn't realize that Abba wanted to be a part of his daily interactions, decisions, and experiences, and he didn't allow Him complete access to every area of his life. His only communication with Abba came when he was in trouble or wanted something from Him. Jacob never took time to seek Abba out just because of who He was.

> *If we are ever going to dwell in Bethel, we must learn how to completely give ourselves to Abba and communicate with Him at all times—not only when we are in trouble, or asking Him to do something for us!*

The key to dwelling in Bethel is continual communication with Abba about every aspect of our lives. It involves Him listening to us when we talk to Him, and us listening and obeying Him when He speaks to us. It is our communication with Him throughout our journey and our obedience that brings us into the promises that He has for us.

Jacob's experiences and encounters during his journey produced a hunger for him to establish a covenant with the God of his father and grandfather, a God who is faithful to His promises. Throughout his life, Jacob had received promises by way of deception; and now, because of his experiences on his journey back to Bethel, he had established a relationship with a God who desired for him to receive the promises He established for him, and to live out his God-ordained destiny, requiring nothing from him but his obedience.

> *Superintendent Lowell T. James, the pastor of Anderson Memorial Church of God in Christ, once described the promises of God as "guaranteed performances." He reminds us that "When God makes a promise, it is for an appointed time and an appointed place. It goes ahead of the receiver and waits so that when the receiver gets to the appointed place, the promise is there."*

The Promise of Protection

In **Genesis 28:12-15**, God makes several promises to Jacob, including the promise to protect him wherever he went. The promise of protection went ahead of Jacob, all the way to Haran, and waited for him to arrive, so that while he was there his Uncle Laban and his cousins could do him no harm, even though they desired to.

Getting Back to Bethel

The promise of protection was waiting for him in Gilead, where his Uncle Laban caught up with him, after Jacob had fled from his home. Laban told Jacob, *"I could destroy you, but the God of your father appeared to me last night and warned me, 'Leave Jacob alone!'"* The promise also went to Peniel and protected Jacob from his brother, Esau, during their reconciliation, and then the promise went on to Succoth and Shechem, and waited on Jacob to arrive.

Even though Jacob made the decision to disobey God by going to these places, it did not alter God's promise of protection. **Genesis 35:5** tells us that God sent out a terror and it spread to all the people surrounding them, and no one attacked Jacob. It was the natural process of seeing God's Word being made manifest in his life that opened Jacob's spiritual eyes so that he could see that the *God of his father and grandfather really is who He appears to be.*

Because Jacob's entire life was built on deception, he assumed that the outcome of his relationship with God would be like every other relationship in his life, which meant that "he had to deceive God before God could deceive him." Jacob had been living his entire life behind a veil of deception and lies, which caused him to assume that everyone he dealt with operated under the same spirit. Jacob learned through the experiences that he had during his journey of getting back to Bethel that there is no deception in God, and He is a keeper of His promises. Jacob's journey allowed him to cultivate a relationship with God that was based on spirit and truth, and his experiences allowed him to understand that God was (and is!) a promise-keeper, and that he could trust Him. He told his family, *"We are going to Bethel, where I will build an altar to the God who answered my prayers when I was in distress. He has been with me wherever I have gone."* **Genesis 35:3 (NLT)**

Jacob's journey was necessary for God to remove everything that was inside of him that was not a part of his destiny: Things that had attached themselves to him through the relationships in his life, his surroundings, and his opinion of himself. It was only after all the idols were removed, the garments were changed, and he purified himself that Jacob was able to go to Bethel. *Just as this was necessary for Jacob, so it is also necessary for us.*

Getting back to Bethel requires us to purge ourselves from the fleshy covenant with the spirit of religion and enter a new covenant with God, filled with expectation of the fulfillment of His promises. According to **2 Corinthians 3:8-12**, we are to expect a greater glory under the new covenant; now that the Holy Spirit is giving life and that if the old way (which brings condemnation) was glorious, how much more glorious is the new way, which makes us right with God. Even though our previous interactions with God produced some wonderful experiences, they do not compare to the glorious encounters that we will now experience dwelling in Bethel.

Time for Reflection…

-"The key to dwelling in Bethel is constant communication with Abba, in every aspect of our lives." There is an old hymn that says, in part, *"Oh, what peace we often forfeit, Oh, what needless pain we bear. All because we do not carry everything to God in prayer."* Do you take everything to Him in prayer? Are there things in your life that you think "This is too small—He surely wouldn't want to be bothered with my little troubles." Why do you feel this way?

-Have you accepted what Jesus did for you on the cross? Do you have the assurance of dwelling with Him forever? If you have not, here is a simple prayer that you can pray, wherever you are.

"Abba Father, thank you for opening my spiritual eyes up to the journey I have experienced thus far. I know that you are calling me to Bethel, the place where you dwell, so I confess with my mouth that I am a sinner, and I believe in my heart that you sent your son, Jesus Christ, to die for me and cleanse me from all of my sins. I ask for your forgiveness, Father, so that I may dwell with you in Bethel forever. Amen."

If you prayed that prayer just now, will you tell someone, so that they can rejoice with you in your new life?

Conclusion

When we dwell in any other location other than Bethel, we stay in a relationship of bondage that is purely performance-based. Because of what Jesus did for us when He died on the cross and then rose up from the grave, we now have the same opportunity as Jacob did; to dwell in Bethel, the house of God. Because of the indwelling of the Holy Spirit, we now have access to a relationship with Abba Father that goes beyond speaking in tongues and is engulfed in the very presence of the great I AM. The idols have been removed, we've been purified, our garments have been changed, and the blessing of Abba, the Father, is upon us to fulfill our God-ordained destiny to be fruitful and multiply by leading others through their journey. Welcome to Bethel—the place where God dwells!

About the Author

Dietra Howard-Sherman is a wife, a mother of four, grandmother of one, and mentor. She resides in the city of Alachua, Florida, where she is the director of Pattie-Cake Christian Academy, a daycare which she co-owns and operates with her husband, Gregory Sherman. She is called by God to the office of Prophet, and is a licensed Evangelist in the Church of God in Christ. Dietra is an active member of Anderson Memorial COGIC in High Springs, Florida, which is under the leadership of Superintendent Lowell T. James and District Missionary Brenda James. Her heart is so intertwined with those who have not yet discovered their worth, especially young girls and women, that it compels her to share the good, bad, and ugly experiences of her life with the power and authority that God has given her so that she can, through the love of Christ and the Word of God, birth them into their God-given destinies.

Contact the Author

Dietra Howard
www.dietrahoward.com
dietradhoward@gmail.com

www.ingramcontent.com/pod-product-compliance
Lightning Source LLC
Chambersburg PA
CBHW052105070526
44584CB00017B/2350